ONE-MINUTE MEDITATIONS

COME AWAY MY BELOVED

FROM THE
BELOVED BOOKS OF
FRANCES J. ROBERTS

BARBOUR
PUBLISHING

© 2008 by Frances J. Roberts

Editorial assistance by Donna Maltese.

ISBN 978-1-60260-213-7

All scripture quotations are taken from the King James Version of the Bible.

Published by Barbour Publishing, Inc., P.O. Box 719, Uhrichsville, Ohio 44683, www.barbourbooks.com

Our mission is to publish and distribute inspirational products offering exceptional value and biblical encouragement to the masses.

 Member of the
Evangelical Christian
Publishers Association

Printed in China.

A MINUTE A DAY CAN CHANGE YOUR LIFE.

We're all busy and pressed for time. But somewhere in our daily schedule, there must be at least sixty free seconds.

Look for that open minute and fill it with this book. *365 One-Minute Meditations from Come Away My Beloved Journal* provides a quick but powerful reading for every day of the year, promising real spiritual impact. Each day's entry features a carefully selected verse from God's Word, along with a condensed reading from *Come Away My Beloved* or other work of Frances J. Roberts, with lines for journaling what's on your heart.

Come Away My Beloved was "forged in the crucible of life," Mrs. Roberts writes, as a book of encouragement, hope, comfort, and conviction for each day's joys and trials. Self-published for many years, *Come Away*, and its companion books from which this book is drawn, have sold more than one and a half million copies.

If you're seeking a spiritual lift, try *365 One-Minute Meditations from Come Away My Beloved Journal*. You'll only need a moment per day—but the benefits could be life changing.

I Seek to Lift Your Load

Humble yourselves in the sight of the Lord, and he shall lift you up.
JAMES 4:10

Seek Me early; seek Me late; seek Me in the midst of the day. You need Me in the early hours for direction and guidance and for My blessing upon your heart. You need Me at the end of the day to commit into My hands the day's happenings. And you need Me more than ever in the busy hours, so that I may give you My grace and My tranquility and My wisdom.

I desire to take the tensions of life from you.

from Come Away My Beloved

The Comfort of My Presence

*For thou wilt light my candle: the LORD my God will enlighten my darkness
. . . . By my God have I leaped over a wall.*
PSALM 18:28–29

More than all the comforts of the world, I want you to know the comfort of My presence.

Many dangers beset your path, but I shall keep you if you trust in Me. Darkness presses you, and doubts arise, but the light of My Holy Spirit ever burns within your heart to cheer you and encourage you to go on, yes, to go on knowing surely I will bring you out.

from On the Highroad of Surrender

January 3

Take the Glory with You

Walk as children of light.
EPHESIANS 5:8

*B*ehold, I have brought you out of a dark and solitary land. I have given you a drink from My own hand. I delight in your companionship. For I have seen your devotion, and I have observed with pleasure your thoughtfulness to those less fortunate who have crossed your path.

Take the glory of the mountaintop with you; take My presence, My light, My love. This is not the valley of personal darkness—this is the valley where you will find those who need the touch of blessing you can bring.

from *Come Away My Beloved*

_____

_____

_____

_____

January 4

There Is Always an Alternative

And he said, Take. . .thine only son Isaac, whom thou lovest,
and get thee into the land of Moriah; and offer him there.
GENESIS 22:2

*N*o price is too great to pay for the proper care of that which I have given you. Never regard lightly that which is precious in My sight. There is always an alternative to the life of relinquishment, but it is lean and barren. That which is most precious needs to be offered up to Me continually.

My grace is as a beacon. It shall shed light on all that is now obscure.

from *Progress of Another Pilgrim*

_____

_____

_____

_____

A Perpetual Fountain of Glory

I have fought a good fight, I have finished my course, I have kept the faith.
2 Timothy 4:7

Write those things I say to you. Hold back nothing of all I shall say to you. For I shall speak to you in the darkness and shall make your way a path of light. I will cry to you out of the confusion round about, and you shall hear My voice and shall know that which I do.

Look to Me, and I will be your beacon in the night, and you will not stumble over the hidden things.

from *Come Away My Beloved*

Only Yield the Vessel

For as many as are led by the Spirit of God, they are the sons of God.
Romans 8:14

Be obedient to the still, small voice. It will engage your soul in devotion. It will give you direction. It will revive and enlighten your own spirit and imbue your soul with divine love.

I am in your midst, dwelling deep within your being. You need not search for Me any further away than your own heart. The flowing forth of My Spirit shall move through you and speak through you. Only yield your vessel. He is your victory.

from *Progress of Another Pilgrim*

BOUNDLESS JOY

*We have this treasure in earthen vessels, that the excellency
of the power may be of God, and not of us.*
2 CORINTHIANS 4:7

*K*now in your heart that your vessel has been formed for the purpose of shedding abroad the glory of God, and the Spirit ministers in you to the end that this may be accomplished.

Lo, I stand at your side to help, and you shall never need to rely on your own strength or wisdom. As long as you bless and honor Me, the rivers of life shall flow forth and your joy shall be boundless.

from *Progress of Another Pilgrim*

PREPARATION

*I am the LORD thy God which teacheth thee to profit,
which leadeth thee by the way that thou shouldest go.*
ISAIAH 48:17

*N*o event in your life is a mistake. I will use every circumstance to enrich your ministry and perfect your soul. You shall go because I have need of you, and minister in the full power of your calling.

I shall thrust you forth. The opening of doors is My responsibility; but the preparation of your soul is your own responsibility.

If you would be ready when the time comes, be diligent and follow My guidance.

from *Progress of Another Pilgrim*

PRETENSE WILL NOT WORSHIP

The Spirit. . .will guide you into all truth.
JOHN 16:13

*O*ut of much solitude comes a depth of understanding I cannot give to the one who closes himself in with noises to prevent hearing the emptiness of his own soul.

Only prayer furnishes the soul with nourishment; but prayer itself must be born of singleness of heart. Pretense will not enter the gate of worship. Better to be a sinner and confess it than to profess purity you do not possess.

Search your heart in the light of My Word. Let the Holy Spirit give insight.

from On the Highroad of Surrender

SPIRITUAL LIBERTY

Go in to possess the land, which the LORD your God giveth you.
JOSHUA 1:11

*A*n entire generation perished because of indecision, for though they were bodily freed, they never wakened to their spiritual liberty; they grieved the spirit of God for forty years and died in the wilderness, never having received the promise (Hebrews 3:15–19).

Bringing you out, My children, is only the beginning. I am preparing a people who shall go in. They shall possess the land. They shall be strong in the Lord, and they shall fulfill My purposes (Joshua 1).

from On the Highroad of Surrender

BE NOT AFRAID OF SOLITUDE

But the anointing which ye have received of him abideth in you,
and ye need not that any man teach you.
1 JOHN 2:27

I have a ministry for you. You have not found it yet because you have been earnestly and in sincerity and with humble heart trying to conform to the patterns of others.

Be not afraid of solitude. You will not lose My touch. You will not miss a blessing. How shall the hand of any other bring you greater joy or clearer insight than I can bring to you Myself?

from *Progress of Another Pilgrim*

January 12

SEEK ME IN THE HIDDEN PLACES

God hath revealed them unto us by his Spirit: for the Spirit
searcheth all things, yea, the deep things of God.
1 CORINTHIANS 2:10

*U*nderstanding comes not by outer observation but by inner revelation. I Myself will teach you. I Myself will open to you many mysteries. Fret not, neither set a limit as to what you may attain. I will communicate with you more and more, and at a deeper level of understanding, as you seek Me in the hidden places of your soul.

from *Progress of Another Pilgrim*

Constancy

Yea, the darkness hideth not from thee.
PSALM 139:12

*D*o not let your heart be discouraged. I am nearer you than ever in the past. I have brought you up to a place of constancy, and I will hold you firm regardless of what you are feeling.

You do not need always to see My face to know I am near. You may touch My face to know I am near. You may touch My hand by faith in moments when it is too dark to see anything. My Spirit is everywhere. . .even in the darkness.

from *On the Highroad of Surrender*

Hold Your Ground

Let us go up at once, and possess it; for we are well able to overcome it.
NUMBERS 13:30

I have not brought you out of the wilderness to allow you to be devoured by the giants in the land. I brought you out by a miracle and I bring you in that you may experience My delivering power.

Stretch forth the hand of faith. Set foot upon the territory you wish to claim. I will move ahead of you and clear a path, but you must be determined to follow closely, and to hold your ground without wavering.

from *On the Highroad of Surrender*

January 15

A Spirit of Gratitude

Every place that the sole of your foot shall tread upon,
that have I given unto you.
JOSHUA 1:3

*T*he path has been prepared before you, and you shall not fear, neither hesitate. As you tread, you will find the victory has already been won. No challenge shall turn you aside, no past defeat shall dim your faith in My provision and grace.

Love Me with your whole heart. I am the Lord, your God. I have saved you and healed you, and you have much for which to praise Me. Never cease to keep a spirit of overflowing gratitude.

from *Progress of Another Pilgrim*

_____

_____

_____

_____

January 16

Rejoice Always

Rejoice in the Lord always.
PHILIPPIANS 4:4

*B*e obedient to My command that you rejoice in the Lord always. Because I must become your one true source of life and joy, I allow the difficult circumstances to come. Through them, I test your love for Me. My love for you is constant and is not to be reckoned by your own happiness or unhappiness. If you have unhappiness, it is because of your own wrong reactions.

Learn to react rightly and properly discern My intention. Never blame Me for your misery, for it is not from My hand.

from *On the Highroad of Surrender*

_____

_____

_____

_____

RECOGNIZE MY HAND

He brought me forth. . .into a large place.
2 SAMUEL 22:20

I have assured you that there would be a reward for your faithfulness. You are now at a place where you can already lift up your eyes and look upon it. I have prepared this for you, and I have stood beside you through the times of endurance. I have urged you on when you would have given up, because I would not allow you to fail. Recognize My hand in this. Your work is My work, and I am well able to take care of every aspect.

from Progress of Another Pilgrim

SATURATE YOUR SOUL IN THE OIL OF THE SPIRIT

We are troubled on every side, yet not distressed;
we are perplexed, but not in despair.
2 CORINTHIANS 4:8

The everlasting power of the Godhead is incarnate in My chosen ones. Is it not written that the kingdom of God dwells within you? I will bring to pass miracles—when you walk in uprightness and with mercy.

Come to Me with a clean heart and a right spirit, in sincerity, in honesty. Saturate your soul in the oil of the Holy Spirit, and keep your channel of communication always open to your Heavenly Father.

from Come Away My Beloved

YOU SHALL NOT BE EARTHBOUND

Where thou lodgest, I will lodge.
RUTH 1:16

*M*ount up on the wings of My power. For there are powers of the air to be subdued and conquered. You need faith and the liberty and power of the Holy Spirit to overcome these and rise above them.

My Church shall be an overcoming church, and My Bride shall be a heavenly being. I will take to Me one who has chosen to make My home her home, even as Ruth did. But she who turns back, like Orpah, shall not enter into My inheritance.

from Come Away My Beloved

I ANTICIPATE YOUR DEPENDENCE ON ME

Nevertheless I live; yet not I, but Christ liveth in me.
GALATIANS 2:20

*D*o not wait to feel worthy, for no one is worthy of My blessings. My grace bypasses your shortcomings, and I give to My children because they ask of Me and because I love them. I give most liberally to those who ask the most of Me.

As you open your heart to Me, I will come to you. As you speak to Me, I will speak to you. As you reveal yourself to Me, I will reveal Myself to you.

from Come Away My Beloved

I WILL SHARE MY SECRETS

He revealeth the deep and secret things.
DANIEL 2:22

I will share with you My secrets
And reveal the hidden thing.
I will lift you out of darkness—
Understanding will I bring.
If you seek Me in My fulness
And desire to know My heart,
I will open heaven's riches
And My wisdom I'll impart.

from *Make Haste My Beloved*

SET YOUR HEART TO FOLLOW TO THE END

He that soweth to the Spirit shall of the Spirit reap life everlasting.
GALATIANS 6:8

My Name is above every Name, and praise and glory belong to Me, and in Me every living thing shall rejoice. For I will cause a light to shine out of the darkness, and in that place where you have walked in defeat, there I will cause victory to break forth.

Rise, arise, and put on your strength, for you are a people called by My Name, and in My Name you will be strong and accomplish great things. And I will bless you.

from *Come Away My Beloved*

ONE-MINUTE MEDITATIONS

January 23

INNER CALM

Acquaint now thyself with him, and be at peace:
thereby good shall come unto thee.
JOB 22:21

*L*et nothing disturb your quietness of spirit, for from the place of inner calm you draw courage to move forward through all obstacles. I am never the source of turbulence. You may react with turbulence when I am dealing with your soul, but whenever you do so, it is because your will is in rebellion and you have stiffened your neck. My disciplines are received with peace in the heart that is submissive to My will.

from *On the Highroad of Surrender*

January 24

THE CENTRAL OBJECT

But whosoever drinketh of the water that I shall give him shall never thirst.
JOHN 4:14

*Y*ou shall hunger forever if you do not learn to feed on Me. Your thirst shall never be quenched except you drink of the Spirit and partake of the Christ life. No mortal shall bless you thus.

Your heart shall rejoice when I am the central object of your affection. Dedication brings pure rapture when the desire is wholly fixed upon Me! My Name alone, when breathed in adoration, lifts the weariest heart from despair and fills the seeking soul with exhilaration.

from *Progress of Another Pilgrim*

PRAISE TRANSFORMS

In every thing give thanks.
1 THESSALONIANS 5:18

ejoice in Me always, for as you rejoice and give thanks, you release heaven's treasures and shower upon your head the blessings of a delighted Father. Nothing so thoroughly delights the Father's heart as the praises of His children.

For praise inclines the heart toward gratitude, and gratitude nurtures contentment, and you may know for a certainty that no fruit ever appears on the tree of discontent.

So never cease in your praising, for in the midst of it I will manifest Myself. Praise will transform the humblest dwelling to a hallowed haven.

from *On the Highroad of Surrender*

HEAVEN'S GIFT

January 26

My people shall dwell in a peaceable habitation, and in sure dwellings, and in quiet resting places.
ISAIAH 32:18

uietness of soul, My child, is heaven's rarest gift enjoyed aforetime. To abide in Me is to know release from tensions; and the ear that is attuned to My voice does not respond to chaos.

People assault their ears with noise to drown the cry of their souls for help. All too often they choose to perpetuate their own misery rather than repent of their evil ways and accept the rulership of another who is greater than themselves.

from *On the Highroad of Surrender*

SUBMISSION AND REDEMPTION

Behold, I have refined thee, but not with silver;
I have chosen thee in the furnace of affliction.
ISAIAH 48:10

*D*eath is swallowed up in victory only for the man who has committed fully into the hands of the Father his total being.

Trust Me now, as I do My perfecting work.

Lean upon My heart. I take no pleasure in afflicting your soul. I desire always for you a speedy deliverance. You help to bring it as you trust Me and as you yield your soul to My work in you (Romans 7:24–25).

from *Progress of Another Pilgrim*

AS RAINS OF REFRESHING

Humble yourselves. . .under the mighty hand of God, that he may exalt you in due time.
1 PETER 5:6

*D*o not be anxious concerning tomorrow. You shall encounter nothing of which I am not already aware. My mercy is concealed within every storm cloud. My grace flows beneath every crosscurrent.

The storm is not a thing to fear but rather to welcome. As soon as you have made the discovery that in the time of stress and strain you have the clearest revelations of Myself, you will learn to head into the wind with sheer delight.

from *Come Away My Beloved*

HE HAS FILLED MY CUP

He said. . .As captain of the host of the LORD am I now come.
And Joshua fell on his face.
JOSHUA 5:14

I stand before you as the Mighty Captain
   of the Hosts of the Almighty,
And you as men of war. (See Joshua 5:13–15.)
   Seek no longer
To rest in green pastures and lie beside still waters;
   For I have issued my command to wipe
     out the giants,
   And to utterly destroy the inhabitants of the land.

from *Come Away My Beloved*

MY ENERGIZING SPIRIT

January 30

The city had no need of the sun, neither of the moon, to shine in it:
for the glory of God did lighten it, and the Lamb is the light thereof.
REVELATION 21:23

*M*y child, I will help thee. I am more real than all thy desires or thy fears. My Spirit is a quickening, life-giving Spirit. I come to be thy Light.

Surely if I can brighten all of Eternity, I have ample supply to flood thy heart and mind and thy body with My mighty power, My light, and My love—My deep joy and My energizing Spirit.

from *Dialogues with God*

January 31

THE CALL OF LOVE

My beloved. . .looketh forth at the windows,
shewing himself through the lattice.
SONG OF SOLOMON 2:9

O My beloved, abide under the shelter of the lattice for I have betrothed you to Myself, and though you are sometimes indifferent toward Me, My love for you is at all times as a flame of fire. My ardor never cools.

Tarry not for an opportunity to have more time to be alone with Me. Take it, though you leave the tasks at hand. Nothing will suffer. Things are of less importance than you think.

from *Come Away My Beloved*

February 1

THE BURDEN-BEARER

He might prove thee, to do thee good at thy latter end.
DEUTERONOMY 8:16

My child, do not share your burdens with all who come to you professing concern. I, Myself, am the great burden-bearer. You need not look to another. I will lead you and guide you in wisdom from above. All things will be as I plan them, if you allow Me the freedom to shape circumstances and lead you to the right decisions.

from *Come Away My Beloved*

Find Solitude

O Lord of hosts, if thou wilt. . .give unto thine handmaid a man child,
then I will give him unto the Lord all the days of his life.
1 SAMUEL 1:11

There is no blessing I would withhold from those who walk in obedience to Me. Near to My heart and precious in My sight are those who have eyes to discern My purpose and ears that listen to My direction.

Do not be intent on great accomplishments. It was a relatively small thing that Hannah prayed for a son, but what great things I accomplished through Samuel!

from *Come Away My Beloved*

The Bent of the Soul

Do all in the name of the Lord Jesus.
COLOSSIANS 3:17

I am in business as surely as I am in the sanctuary of worship. In fact, the former becomes the proving ground of the latter.

Your own inner consecration hallows the outer action. Two may do what appears to be the same work. The difference is in the bent of the soul whether it be for the glory of God or for self-aggrandizement. I breathe My very life into that which is offered to Me as a sacrifice of love.

from *On the Highroad of Surrender*

INDOLENCE

*The field of the slothful. . .was all grown over with thorns. . .
and the stone wall thereof was broken down.*
PROVERBS 24:30–31

*Y*ou could easily fill your days with frivolous or selfish pursuits. Guard your time and energies, as they are the material from which the spiritual ministries are of necessity channeled. Dissipate your physical strength, or carelessly waste your time, and thus shall the Spirit be thwarted. Simple indolence is by itself a militant force against the Spirit. Resist it in the full recognition of the destructive power that it is.

from *Progress of Another Pilgrim*

ON COPING WITH SUCCESS

*Whosoever hath, to him shall be given. . .but whosoever hath not,
from him shall be taken away even that he hath.*
MATTHEW 13:12

*B*e never entangled by thoughts concerning the reactions of others to your ministry. Minister, and follow the leading of the Spirit. Search your heart, and pray for the strength to receive great results.

I may withhold blessings because I foresee your own unreadiness to receive. Learn how to prepare your mind and heart to cope with success, otherwise when it comes you may by your very unreadiness undo the good that has been done.

from *On the Highroad of Surrender*

RELEASE YOUR TENSIONS

The work of righteousness shall be peace;
and the effect of righteousness quietness and assurance for ever.
ISAIAH 32:17

*W*hen you are rebuffed and bear it patiently, yes, even in the moment when it appears as though the actions of others prevent the fulfillment of your own inner vision, be assured, My child, of My understanding and patience, and know that I am a harmonizing influence.

I have a unique plan for each life, and as you release to Me your tensions, you can rely on Me to continue My work in each soul and bring it ultimately to perfection.

from On the Highroad of Surrender

_____

_____

_____

_____

_____

_____

SPEAK THE TRUTH

Be strong in the Lord, and in the power of his might.
EPHESIANS 6:10

*D*o not be intimidated by anyone, but speak forth My Word as I give it to you.

You are not pleasing Me but trying to please men. They will detect your inconsistency in spite of your best efforts, for in one way or another, the truth will break through. You need not say all that is in your heart, but you must either speak the truth or be silent.

Let the life and witness of Jesus Christ be your guide.

from Come Away My Beloved

_____

_____

_____

_____

_____

February 8

MOTIVATION

If my people. . .humble themselves, and pray, and seek my face,
and turn from their wicked ways; then will I hear from heaven,
and will forgive their sin, and will heal their land.
2 CHRONICLES 7:14

Confession, repentance, and prayer strengthen the will to move in the direction of holiness. No one is brought into a life of holiness by outside force. The inner desire is always the first and the foremost motivation. As soon as the desire for righteousness is present, the Holy Spirit will immediately fill it with His own energy and bring the soul into victory.

from *Progress of Another Pilgrim*

February 9

STRENGTHENING POWER

What I would, that do I not; but what I hate, that do I.
ROMANS 7:15

You need the daily inward strengthening of the new man in the power of My might, to be enabled to walk in obedience to My commands.

You know to do good but continually battle the tendencies of your human nature to do otherwise. For the flesh resisteth the progress of the Spirit (Romans 7:15–25). But as Paul, you make your confession: Thanks be to God, which giveth us the victory through our Lord Jesus Christ!

from *Dialogues with God*

A MERRY HEART

A merry heart doeth good like a medicine.
PROVERBS 17:22

*N*othing is gained, but much is lost by bitterness of spirit in the day of trouble. You may not be able to escape calamity, but you should even more avoid a doleful countenance because it denotes a tempest in the heart and turbulence of mind, and reveals rebellion against the hand of God as it shapes destiny.

Look unto Jesus, "the author and finisher of our faith" (Hebrews 12:2). Peace, joy, and hope are His mantle, and holiness emanates from His presence.

from *On the Highroad of Surrender*

YOU SHALL NOT BE EARTHBOUND

February 11

The water that I shall give him shall be in him a well of water
springing up into everlasting life.
JOHN 4:14

*W*hatever you need, if you will look to Me, I will supply.

I will surround you and preserve you, so that in Me you may live, move, and have your being, existing in Me when apart from Me you would die.

You will live in a realm where the things of earth will not be able to limit your movement; but you will be freed in Me to a place where your spirit may soar as the eagle.

from *Come Away My Beloved*

LIBERTY

Those that walk in pride he is able to abase.
DANIEL 4:37

Stand fast in the liberty wherein I have made you free and allow no one to move you into a position of compromise. Be diligent to make the most of the opportunities thus afforded you.

You will never discover what I have planned for you if in your zeal you run ahead and become again entangled. I free you and I want to keep you free. Why do you look to others for help when I am already at work moving mountains on your behalf?

Be at peace.

from On the Highroad of Surrender

HOLD FAST

Looking unto Jesus the author and finisher of our faith.
HEBREWS 12:2

Hold fast that which you have, and let no one take your crown.

Let no one hinder you in pursuit of the reward. Let nothing stand in the way of your complete victory.

Let no weariness or discouraging thought cause you to loosen the rope of faith, but bind it tighter and anchor fast to My Word.

My Word can never fail.

from Come Away My Beloved

To Feel Need Is to Receive Grace

Call unto me, and I will answer thee, and show thee
great and mighty things, which thou knowest not.
JEREMIAH 33:3

*N*o obstacle within yourself can restrict My grace. I use many vessels while they are struggling with their failures; for in their conscious sense of need, they are more yielded to Me than they who think themselves to be without flaw.

To feel need is to receive grace. The mighty things which you do not comprehend are the miraculous things I do for you and through you in your acknowledged times of need.

from *Make Haste My Beloved*

Adversity

In every thing give thanks.
1 THESSALONIANS 5:18

*W*hen you do not strive against adversity, its power to hurt you is destroyed. The flesh may suffer, but the spirit will be blessed.

My voice speaks through every situation to the ear that is yielded to the Spirit. My love flows freely through every sorrow to the heart that is devoted to Me. I will not fail anyone resting and trusting in My goodness.

Evils pass as ships in the night when peace reigns in the surrendered soul. Leave with Me every unsolved problem. Rejoice while I work it all out.

from *Progress of Another Pilgrim*

February 16

FAITH AND THE DELIVERING ANGEL

Thy servant slew both the lion and the bear:
and this uncircumcised Philistine shall be as one of them.
1 SAMUEL 17:36

I slew the lion and the bear," said David, and having thus developed courage, he moved unflinchingly to confront the giant Philistine. That which had been tried in solitude broke into evidence in the public crisis. It was in this area of faith and courage that he was above his fellows.

Secret faith had its moment of open revelation. Build inner faith from the lesser challenges, and it will be your delivering angel in the most calamitous moment.

from *Progress of Another Pilgrim*

February 17

MINISTERING ANGELS

Be careful for nothing; but in every thing by prayer and supplication
with thanksgiving let your requests be made known unto God.
PHILIPPIANS 4:6

*B*e anxious for nothing.

Always turn to Me before you look to any other source of assistance. My love will light your path, so that you may be guided in finding other help. I have given you ministering angels, who may sometimes come to you in the form of your friends. Accept their help as from Me, and your blessing will be doubled. You may also, in turn, be used in similar manner to bless others.

from *Come Away My Beloved*

The Glory Life

For my thoughts are not your thoughts,
neither are your ways my ways, saith the Lord.
Isaiah 55:8

Thou knowest not the direction of thyself, but it shall be revealed unto thee by My Spirit, saith the Lord. Day by day and step by step, thou shalt walk by faith, not by thine own cunningly devised plans.

Question Me not, nor ask Me why, neither put confidence in the wisdom of thine own thoughts.

from *Dialogues with God*

_____
_____
_____
_____
_____

Prepare!

February 19

And God said unto Noah. . .Make thee an ark of gopher wood.
Genesis 6:13–14

Your own future is shaped by today's decisions, therefore the future should not be ignored as though irrelevant to today. Jesus did not teach man to ignore the future, but to prepare for it. His warning was against anxiety concerning tomorrow, not against preparation.

It was I who taught Noah to prepare for the flood. Draw on My wisdom, for to Me all things are plain now.

from *Make Haste My Beloved*

_____
_____
_____
_____
_____

SPIRITUAL AWARENESS

We have received, not the spirit of the world, but the spirit which is of God;
that we might know the things. . .of God.
1 CORINTHIANS 2:12

*A*s a child has eyesight, but only by teaching and study does he learn the art of reading, so likewise, what I do for you is to train you to comprehend intelligently that which you see in the Spirit.

The same principle applies in the other areas of spiritual awareness. Let Me be your teacher and guide you into how to interpret the information that comes to you.

from *Progress of Another Pilgrim*

_____

_____

_____

_____

_____

_____

February 21

A YIELDED, BELIEVING VESSEL

But the people that do know their God shall be strong, and do exploits.
DANIEL 11:32

*M*ine is the wisdom and the honor and the power and the glory.

I am never defeated, but My justice and My mercy are obstructed by human ignorance and by the lack of faith.

Be aware of Me. I can accomplish great things through even one yielded, believing vessel. Remember David, and how I wrought a great victory for the armies of Israel through his courage when all others were paralyzed by fear.

Move on, and never entertain the thought of retreat.

from *Come Away My Beloved*

_____

_____

_____

_____

_____

Warring in the Spirit

They overcame him by the blood of the Lamb,
and by the word of their testimony.
REVELATION 12:11

*O*nly the one who is taught of the Spirit can war in the Spirit. You must war, because there are enemies unseen to human eyes but constantly besieging the child of God. But he is not left defenseless. Heavenly protection is his as well as offensive weapons. The sword of the Spirit, the blood of the Lamb, and the word of testimony are provided for every saint of God, but must be put into action in faith before they can bring about a deliverance.

from *On the Highroad of Surrender*

Faith Manifesting in Divine Response   February 23

My God hath sent his angel, and hath shut the lions' mouths, that they have not hurt me.
DANIEL 6:22

*N*o evil can hurt you if you yield it up to Me, because as you do so, I bring to bear upon it forces of good. One example in the Bible is the visitation of angels for the preservation of Daniel. The power of righteousness at work within the heart of Daniel brought to his aid the protecting forces. It was faith and committal manifesting into divine response.

The same law will work for you. Test it and prove it.

from *Progress of Another Pilgrim*

TESTINGS

*That the trial of your faith, being much more precious
than of gold that perisheth, though it be tried with fire, might be found
unto praise and honour and glory at the appearing of Jesus Christ.*

1 PETER 1:7

*I*n a multitude of testings I would perfect your understanding. I am not unaware of the pressures thus inflicted upon you, but as the trials come and go, I not only turn them into a means of blessing, but I never fail to make available My comfort and My sustaining strength.

from *Progress of Another Pilgrim*

I DO NOT SEND STORMS

There is no peace. . .to the wicked.

ISAIAH 57:21

*D*ear Jesus, in the hollow of Thy hand there is peace.

Do not ask Me to give you peace when you have removed yourself from My hand or if you are unwilling to rest quietly there. I give My peace to all who love and serve Me with singleness of heart.

I do not send storms upon your soul. They are generated by the pressures of your disobedience.

Only in repentance shall My people find peace, and only in singleness of heart shall they find joy.

from *Progress of Another Pilgrim*

CONTENTMENT

Many are the afflictions of the righteous:
but the LORD delivereth him out of them all.
PSALM 34:19

*B*e patient in tribulation and I will minister My grace to you and your heart will rejoice. For when outer blessings are withheld, inner peace is deepened, for the soul turns to worship with less distraction.

Disappointment is foreign to the Spirit, for it has no part in faith. The trusting soul possesses all things in Christ and looks not to others for blessing: therefore he can never be disappointed. Joy and contentment crown his head, and peace reigns in his heart.

from *On the Highroad of Surrender*

PERSEVERANCE, THE ANGEL OF LOVE
February 27

Praying always.
EPHESIANS 6:18

*P*erseverance is the rope that ties the soul to the doorpost of heaven. Not to give up in face of the impossible is humanity's ultimate salvation. It is well called "the perseverance of the saints," for it requires saintly determination to continue on in dedication when all the forces of hell are arrayed against the soul.

Perseverance is to the human spirit what the rudder is to a ship. It will steer the ship dead ahead in spite of the contrary wind. You must have holy determination, pressing on in defiance of all odds.

from *On the Highroad of Surrender*

365
ONE-MINUTE MEDITATIONS

February 28

DELIVERANCE HAS COME

And when they began to sing and to praise, the LORD set ambushments against [their enemies].
2 CHRONICLES 20:22

I have set ambushments against your enemies, and I will smite him that causes you to dwell in fear. I will not suffer your foot to be moved but will cause you to walk in the way I have designed for you and no man shall hinder. For I have set My battle in array, and I the Lord your God will fight for you and you shall hold your peace.

Rejoice, for your deliverance has already come!

from *Make Haste My Beloved*

February 29

VITAL CONTACT

Praying in the Holy Ghost, keep yourselves in the love of God.
JUDE 20–21

*L*ive in constant communion with Me, and strive to maintain continual vital contact. So shall be generated within you the spiritual power which builds up a ready supply for the moments of actual ministry.

This is the reason Jesus spent long hours in lonely vigil with His Father. This is why the Scriptures admonish you to pray without ceasing.

As you pray and meditate, you are enriched by the Spirit in the grace and compassion of Jesus Christ.

from *Progress of Another Pilgrim*

Outer Blessing and Inner Strength

Caleb, because he had another spirit with him,
and hath followed me fully, him will I bring into the land.
NUMBERS 14:24

*P*onder for a moment what great crises would face you if tomorrow all your prayers were answered! Could you bear the new joy—the added responsibility? Therefore, when you pray, ask not only for the desired results, but also that your heart will be strengthened to receive, and that added wisdom be given to meet the new problems.

You have watched some succeed only to fail. This occurs when outer blessings are sought and inner strength neglected.

from *On the Highroad of Surrender*

Devotion and Warfare

March 2

For the builders, every one had his sword girded by his side,
and so builded. And he that sounded the trumpet was by me.
NEHEMIAH 4:18

*P*resume not to labor to build with the right hand without holding the sword in the left (Nehemiah 4:18). It is vigilance combined with prayer that spells victory. Devotion must be coupled with warfare to be fruitful. Holy ecstasy must be mixed with holy boldness, and love must be blended with courage. Only to pray is not enough. Prayer must rise from the battlefield of spiritual conquest.

from *On the Highroad of Surrender*

March 3

YOU SHALL MOVE SWIFTLY

Be careful for nothing; but in every thing by prayer. . .
let your requests be made known unto God.
PHILIPPIANS 4:6

I will make My will known to you, and you will no longer move haltingly, you shall move swiftly and surely.

With your hand in Mine, we will move together. My Spirit will be apparent by your life and testimony, and you will be empowered by My might and power.

Be anxious for nothing, but in all situations in prayer and in fasting, bring each emergency case to Me, for I am the Great Physician.

from *Come Away My Beloved*

March 4

FEAR, A SIN

Hebron therefore became the inheritance of Caleb. . .
because that he wholly followed the LORD.
JOSHUA 14:14

*B*e not faint of heart. Fear will rob you of your possession as quickly as any other sin; for truly fear is a sin and it opens the door for many other sins to follow.

Guard your heart from doubt and every negative attitude. You cannot afford to take the risk of entertaining any such thoughts at so critical a time. Only the strong in faith shall prevail. Only those with a "Caleb" spirit shall take the walled cities and crush out the enemies.

from *On the Highroad of Surrender*

YOUR LIFE IS AS A WEAVING

Let the peace of God rule in your hearts.
COLOSSIANS 3:15

*Y*our life is as a weaving. From fabrics of lovely silk and from cords of rougher materials, I fashion what pleases Me. You may never know why certain experiences come. It is enough that My hand brings them all.

My grace is not limited by sorrow and difficulty. Indeed, it shines like a strand of gold mixed in with the black of grief. My hand moves with infinite love, and I am creating a pattern of intricate beauty.

Never be dismayed. For you are My workmanship, created in Christ.

from *Come Away My Beloved*

OBEDIENCE, THE FABRIC OF HAPPINESS

March 6

Ye shall do my judgments, and keep mine ordinances, to walk therein.
LEVITICUS 18:4

*L*ook to Me, My child, and all your needs will be met by My abundant provision. I will not suffer the enemy to overthrow him who puts his confidence in Me. I am faithful to My Word, and I have promised never to fail nor to forsake.

Obedience is the fabric of happiness. To rebel is to seek sorrow. Only a yielded heart can find rest in Me; and to know contentment there must be resignation of personal rights in favor of My will.

from *Make Haste My Beloved*

March 7

LOOK DEEPLY

I taught [the gospel]. . .by the revelation of Jesus Christ.
GALATIANS 1:12

*L*ook deeply within your heart, and much will be revealed. Many things will become clear to you as you look into your innermost being. It is a storehouse of wisdom. Fear it not, for it is a deep pool of divine life because I Myself reside there.

I will teach you in symbols as you learn to see in the Spirit.

Dismiss traditions. Drive out the bondman. Your spirit needs free course for expression. Do not hamper it in ignorance.

from Progress of Another Pilgrim

March 8

A GARDEN OF FOUNTAINS

The LORD shall guide thee continually, and satisfy thy soul in drought. . .
thou shalt be like a watered garden.
ISAIAH 58:11

*M*y hand is upon you to bless you and to accomplish all My good purpose. I will not let you fail.

Only relinquish all things into My hands; for I can work freely only as you release Me by complete committal—both of yourself and others. As was written of old: "Commit thy way unto the LORD, trust also in him; and he shall bring it to pass" (Psalm 37:5).

from Come Away My Beloved

Set Your Course
by My Promises

The Lord is faithful, who shall stablish you, and keep you from evil.
2 Thessalonians 3:3

*B*e not afraid. Because of My faithfulness to you, even your enemies will recognize My power. Hold to My promises. They are given to you as a chart is given to a ship, and a compass to the hunter. You may set your course and find your way by My promises. They will lead you and guide you in places where there is no trodden path.

Study My Word. It abounds with nuggets of courage. It will strengthen you and help you.

from *Come Away My Beloved*

_____

_____

_____

_____

_____

In the Fiery Furnace

*I see four men loose, walking in the midst of the fire, and they have no hurt;
and the form of the fourth is like the Son of God.*
Daniel 3:25

*M*odern man has so protected himself from discomfort that his body and his soul are in a dangerously weakened condition. Where shall he draw courage in the day of affliction?

Always you need My guidance.

Look for Me in the midst of every fiery furnace and you will be influenced by My Spirit rather than by your own natural impulses (2 Corinthians 11:16–33; 2 Timothy 2:3).

from *Progress of Another Pilgrim*

_____

_____

_____

_____

_____

THE COWARD SEEKS RELEASE

And the princes, governors, and captains, and the king's counsellors,
being gathered together, saw these men, upon whose bodies the fire had no power,
nor was an hair of their head singed, neither were their coats changed,
nor the smell of fire had passed on them.
DANIEL 3:27

*H*old fast, My child, for in the hour of anguish, then shall you walk in victory. Do not pray to be brought out of the fire until after you have found Me real in the midst of it.

The coward seeks release from pressure. The courageous pray for strength to overcome.

from *On the Highroad of Surrender*

A WAY OF TRIUMPH

Eye hath not seen, nor ear heard, neither have entered into the heart of man,
the things which God hath prepared for them that love him.
1 CORINTHIANS 2:9

*N*ever be led by human reasoning. The day is coming when you would have faltered but for the understanding I am giving you now.

It is a way of triumph when it leads to fuller enlightenment. When My presence is with you, you can know there is a blessing in store. It shall open to you as you trust Me. It shall be beautiful beyond your highest dreams.

from *Progress of Another Pilgrim*

This Is the Glory Life

*The cloud of the Lord was upon the tabernacle by day,
and fire was on it by night.*
EXODUS 40:38

*B*ehold, I say unto thee, This is the way, walk ye in it,
    neither turn to the right hand nor to the left.
For I shall make the path for thy feet a plain path,
    and light shall be there,
    and there shall be the shining of My glory.
It shall not be the glory of man. It shall be the glory of God.

from *Dialogues with God*

A Devouring Fire

*When the enemy shall come in like a flood, the Spirit of the Lord
shall lift up a standard against him.*
ISAIAH 59:19

*D*arkness is ever moving against My church. It moves against you as a believer, but I have promised to deliver, and he who walks in prayer shields his soul from the enemy.

Hold forth the word of truth, both receiving it and giving it, for it is a devouring fire as it goes forth against evil. You shall be able to scatter much darkness and combat the powers of evil as you speak My Word in faith.

from *On the Highroad of Surrender*

RETURN UNTO ME

*Be not conformed to this world: but be ye transformed
by the renewing of your mind.*
ROMANS 12:2

Return to Me; for I have sought after you, but you have continued on in pursuit of your own ways. I have called to you, but you have disregarded Me. I have placed obstacles in your path, but you have obstinately and determinedly forged on ahead.

Have you learned no wisdom? Have past lessons fled your mind? Put down your anxieties, and trust Me for everything. You need nothing but what I am fully able to supply, with no effort on your part.

from Come Away My Beloved

March 16

GIVE YOURSELF TO PRAYER AND THE WORD

But we will give ourselves continually to prayer, and to the ministry of the word.
ACTS 6:4

Give yourself to a life of prayer and much careful study of the Word.

Dispose of nonessentials. Concentrate your thoughts and intentions upon Jesus Christ, and in Him seek your wisdom and comfort. I will open avenues to aid you, for this is My will for you, and you can know that I will always make a way for the performance of My will in your life once you have set your goal to be obedient to My commands.

from Progress of Another Pilgrim

RELINQUISH YOUR WILL

And God sent me before you. . .to save your lives by a great deliverance.
GENESIS 45:7

*M*y heart is grieved by your independence. How would Joseph have felt if his father and family had remained at home, starving in the famine, when he had invited them to share the bountiful stores he had at his disposal?

I seek not to interfere with your happiness, but I do require that you relinquish your will; for I cannot bless you as I desire to do until your will is yielded up and you accept Mine in exchange.

from *Come Away My Beloved*

ATTITUDE DETERMINES OUTCOME

I was not disobedient unto the heavenly vision.
ACTS 26:19

*I*n every situation, you have a confrontation of duty. You can, by total dedication of your own being, turn every experience into a spiritual victory. It is the attitude with which you approach any day that will determine its outcome.

You are not a helpless pawn on a board. You are a child of God with prerogatives for accomplishing His will, not your own. Let this help to bring you guidance when you are in doubt.

from *On the Highroad of Surrender*

March 19

ETERNITY AND TIME

A wheel in the middle of a wheel.
EZEKIEL 1:16

*D*o not let the sound of war and discords deafen your ears to My message; for I would speak to you a word of encouragement and hope.

Do not focus on the problems of the world; but look up.

My ageless purposes are set in Eternity. Time is like a little wheel set within the big wheel of Eternity. The little wheel turns swiftly and shall one day cease. The big wheel turns not, but goes straightforward. Time is your responsibility—Eternity is Mine!

from Come Away My Beloved

March 20

THE HEADSHIP OF CHRIST

Gird up the loins of your mind, be sober, and hope to the end.
I PETER 1:13

*M*any are looking to you for deliverance and for salvation. Be aware of every possible moment of opportunity. The eternal destiny of lives is at stake. A frivolous spirit or a careless indulgence in levity may rob both yourself and the other person of a priceless experience in the creative power of the Spirit. Don't take such a precarious path. Stay in the Spirit, and keep your mind in captivity to the mind and the thoughts of Christ. Be satisfied with nothing less.

from Progress of Another Pilgrim

Grow Up in Me

The fruit of the Spirit is love, joy, peace, longsuffering, gentleness,
goodness, faith, meekness, temperance.
GALATIANS 5:22–23

*N*ow that you are in Christ, you have My life abiding in you, and you have become a new creation. Grow up in Me now, so that you may develop to the measure of the fullness of Christ (see Ephesians 4:13).

My purpose was not simply to bring you into My family to remain as babies or children. I am concerned with your maturity and with the producing of the fruits of the Spirit in your life.

from *Come Away My Beloved*

I Will Use but Not Destroy You

March 22

My word. . .shall not return unto me void.
ISAIAH 55:11

*O*My child, do not let your energies be consumed by humdrum tasks. What is needed must be done; but if you put the ministry of the Kingdom in first place, My strength will be yours for other tasks, and time will be given to you for both.

Learn to discern when I would use you, and when I would have the other individual lean wholly upon Me.

I will use you, but I will not destroy you in the using.

from *Come Away My Beloved*

March 23

RESPONSIBILITIES AND PRIVILEGES

For unto every one that hath shall be given, and he shall have abundance:
but from him that hath not shall be taken away even that which he hath.
MATTHEW 25:29

Responsibilities always increase in proportion to privileges. He who is recipient of great spiritual riches, of him will I require much in the way of ministry. Let the earthly life of the Lord Jesus be an example to you. Day and night He toiled, praying by night and working by day. So must you.

from *Progress of Another Pilgrim*

March 24

TOTAL RELINQUISHMENT

We have not an high priest which cannot be touched with the feeling of our infirmities.
HEBREWS 4:15

As you ponder the sufferings of the Lord Jesus Christ, you shall gain insight into your own pain. Only in prayer and meditation on the Holy Word can understanding come to your heart, and only thus can you be truly comforted in the Spirit.

Nothing can remain of self-will if My full purpose is to be accomplished. Slowly, unrelentingly, each soul moves to his own Gethsemane of total relinquishment of all his cherished personal hopes and on to his own barren Golgotha.

from *Progress of Another Pilgrim*

UNION OF SPIRIT

I in them, and thou in me.
JOHN 17:23

There is a flow of divine life, and as you enter into it, you shall find victory. If you long to see your own personal wishes subjugated to the will and purposes of God, let your heart be at rest. For this union of your spirit with My Spirit and of your will and My will shall come as simply and easily as rain falling, if you can learn this one secret, that is, how to lose yourself in the flow of My life as I live within you.

from *Progress of Another Pilgrim*

_____

_____

_____

_____

_____

ASK!

The parched ground shall become a pool, and the thirsty land springs of water.
ISAIAH 35:7

If there is dryness within your soul, you need not grieve or chide yourself for being empty. Fill up the empty place with praise. The King will enter and bring His glory.

For the promise of the Father is the gift of the indwelling presence of My Holy Spirit (see Acts 2:38–39).

It is written: "How much more will your heavenly Father give the Holy Spirit to those who ask Him" (Luke 11:13)! Ask, and you shall receive, and your joy shall be full.

from *Come Away My Beloved*

_____

_____

_____

_____

_____

HOUSEHOLD SALVATION

When he seeth the blood upon the lintel, and on the two side posts,
the LORD will pass over. . .your houses.
EXODUS 12:23

I have blessed you out of the bounties of heaven and have not withheld from you what your heart has desired. Yes, and I would do still more. For have I not promised that you and your household should be saved? Wasn't the blood applied to the lintel and the doorposts for the salvation of the entire family?

So renew your energies, and know that I am working with you.

from *Come Away My Beloved*

DO NOT LIE DORMANT

But they that wait upon the LORD shall renew their strength;
they shall mount up with wings as eagles; they shall run, and not be weary;
and they shall walk, and not faint.
ISAIAH 40:31

My child, I need you. Without your active help, I am hampered in My work. You cannot lie idle without hindering the ministry of the Church as a corporate body. Never be dormant. Do not be slothful, neither let yourself fall asleep.

I am with you, and I will help you. Do not become discouraged or weary or fainthearted, and you will reap My rewards.

from *Come Away My Beloved*

HESITATION

I can do all things through Christ which strengtheneth me.
PHILIPPIANS 4:13

I give you strength according to the task, but I give it as you do the work. To hesitate is to become still more weak and timid, for it is a sense of inadequacy that causes you to draw back and fear to move, and this draws your attention to yourself; and because there is never sufficient power within yourself to do the Father's work, any focus on your own strength or ability will soon persuade you that the task is impossible.

from On the Highroad of Surrender

CLEANSE THE SANCTUARY

March 30

My people. . .have forsaken me the fountain of living waters,
and hewed them out. . .broken cisterns, that can hold no water.
JEREMIAH 2:13

I have commanded that you love Me with a whole heart, and that you serve Me with undivided loyalty. You cannot serve two masters. Cleanse the sanctuary, and bring Me your sacrifices with pure hearts and clean hands. I will not despise the sacrifices of contrite hearts.

Although you have strayed, I have not left you. Wherever you turn to Me in love and confession, I am there in the midst of you.

from Come Away My Beloved

My Love Is Coexistent with My Power

He that dwelleth in love dwelleth in God.
1 JOHN 4:16

March 31

*O*My child, I know thy frame and remember that thou art dust, for thus I fashioned thee. But is it not also written that I breathed upon man, and he became a living soul? Said I not that I made him in Mine own image and likeness? Yea, within the house of clay did I place a part of Myself. Without thee would My body be incomplete.

Draw near to My heart; for My love for thee is coexistent with My power.

from Dialogues with God

The Kingdom of Lights

And he said, I beseech thee, shew me thy glory.
EXODUS 33:18

April 1

*D*o not fear darkness: fear God, and He shall be to you a light. The world is enshrouded in darkness, but they who walk in My truth walk in light. My kingdom is a kingdom of light, and clear, purified vessels are the transmitters of My glory in the darkened world. Shine, My children, and darkness shall be scattered as you walk!

from Make Haste My Beloved

THE GLORY OF MY PRESENCE

My peace I give unto you. . . . Let not your heart be troubled,
neither let it be afraid.
JOHN 14:27

*A*ll through the night have I stood watch.
Through the darkness have I set limits for thy protection,
And lo, the enemy cannot break through the lines.
I am in the midst of My people to give them peace.
I shall dine with them at the table,
though countless hosts encamp round about.
I shall cover them with My almighty hand.

from *Dialogues with God*

SACRIFICE, MY STATUS SYMBOL

For whosoever will save his life shall lose it; but whosoever shall lose his life
for my sake and the gospel's, the same shall save it.
MARK 8:35

*O*My children, you behave not as sons and daughters but as strangers. You boast that you serve Me, but in truth you serve your own ego.

You would make Christianity pleasant and acceptable. Your Savior did not find it so. You would make it comfortable and accommodating to your own schedule. He knew nothing of such a false religion.

Do you desire to truly follow Me? Look for the bloodstained prints of My feet.

from *Come Away My Beloved*

April 4

GOD'S HEART

My beloved spake, and said unto me, Rise up, my love,
my fair one, and come away.
SONG OF SOLOMON 2:10

I love you, and if you can always, as it were, feel My pulse beat, you will receive insight that will give you sustaining strength. I bore your sins and I wish to carry your burdens. Lay your head upon My breast and lose yourself in Me. You will experience resurrection life and peace; the joy of the Lord will become your strength; and wells of salvation will be opened within you (see Song of Solomon 2:9–13).

from *Come Away My Beloved*

_____

_____

_____

_____

_____

April 5

THE SINGING HEART

Faith is the substance of things hoped for, the evidence of things not seen.
HEBREWS 11:1

P atience will manifest where hope is nurtured. The singing heart is blind to obstacles and recognizes in all things the loving hand of an all-wise Father. Delays are unnoticed, for the Spirit is not bound by the limitations of outer circumstances. The power of evil to destroy joy is nullified when Christ Himself becomes the one point of attention. In Him all things are possessed now, for faith beholds that which is yet to be as though it were already a reality.

from *On the Highroad of Surrender*

_____

_____

_____

_____

_____

THE MASTER ARTIST

And God saw every thing that he had made, and, behold, it was very good.
GENESIS 1:31

I make no idle strokes. What I do is never haphazard. I am never merely mixing colors out of casual curiosity. My every move is one of vital creativity, and every stroke is part of the whole.

Never be dismayed by apparent incongruity. Never be alarmed by a sudden dash of color seemingly out of context. Say only to your questioning heart, "It is the Infinite wielding His brush; I know He does all things well."

from Come Away My Beloved

THE SIMPLICITY OF OBEDIENCE

April 7

And unto man he said, Behold, the fear of the LORD, that is wisdom;
and to depart from evil is understanding.
JOB 28:28

*Y*ou need not search for answers to the many mysteries of life, but only trust and follow Me in the simplicity of obedience. Understanding will come to you as you walk in obedience.

Make Me your goal, and wisdom shall be given each day as needed. Do not try to reverse the order.

from Progress of Another Pilgrim

April 8

THE RIGHTEOUS REMNANT

There shall they be called the children of the living God.
ROMANS 9:26

*H*ear Me, O My people, and listen to My words. You give attention continually to the words of others. You listen, read, you study and ponder and consider multitudes of words that express only the thoughts of others who, like yourself, are searching for Truth. To search is not evil, but if you desire understanding, come directly to me. Ask of Me. As the Scriptures teach, if any seeks wisdom, let him ask of God, for He gives liberally (James 1:5).

Wait upon Me, and I will clarify things.

from *On the Highroad of Surrender*

April 9

THE ROMANCE OF THE SPIRIT

Blessed are the undefiled in the way. . .that seek him with the whole heart.
PSALM 119:1–2

*T*here is a path of service in which I would lead you. It is a way of romance—the Romance of the Spirit.

My love for you is deeper than you have comprehended. As you are less hampered by the things of the world, I will give you more complete revelations of Myself.

When you have given up everything, we will be able to go forth together, and you will experience an inner power that you were not able to find before.

from *On the Highroad of Surrender*

The Healing Power of Joy

Your sorrow shall be turned into joy.
JOHN 16:20

*D*istress of soul and grief of heart can only bring on destruction of body. Joy alone is a healer, and you can have it in the darkest hour if you will force your soul to rise to Me in worship and adoration.

Bring Me your sorrow, and watch for the sunrise of the resurrection. Wait for it as tulip bulbs anticipate the spring. When the blossoms break through, we do not then turn back to thoughts of winter, but instead, we look ahead to the full joys of the coming summer.

from *Come Away My Beloved*

Turbulence, a Warning Signal

April 11

For as many as are led by the Spirit of God, they are the sons of God.
ROMANS 8:14

*O*ne step at a time, My child. When I lead, there is no confusion. Never let others lead. Your need for confirmation will be answered by the Spirit. Never move into a new situation until you are at peace about it within your own soul. If you sense discord or turbulence, know that there is a spiritual battle already on the scene. Let it be a warning signal. Look for the root of it, and do not blindly forge ahead.

from *On the Highroad of Surrender*

UNSEEN COMPANIONSHIP

Preserve me, O God: for in thee do I put my trust.
PSALM 16:1

April 12

Courage, My child! No hand shall sustain you but Mine own. Hoped you for another? Disappointment awaits every soul not sustained by My love. Never draw from other sources, for when you do, you confuse comfort with strength.

The soul that has been enriched by communion with God will welcome solitude. He will seek not the crowd but the closet, and emerging will never walk alone, for he has always unseen companionship, and whoever joins him on the way will be doubly blessed.

from On the Highroad of Surrender

April 13

TRIBULATION AND STAMINA

This mystery. . .is Christ in you, the hope of glory.
COLOSSIANS 1:27

Only through much prayer can you endure much tribulation. In no other way can the new life in Christ develop and gain stamina.

Be as a child and trust Me implicitly. I will honor your faith and will give you still more.

Do not place restrictions on divine aid by trying to live the Christian life in your own strength. I Myself am your victory. My kingdom shall be forever, but even now it is in your heart whenever you bow to Me as sovereign.

from Make Haste My Beloved

RELEASE OTHERS

But as for you, ye thought evil against me; but God meant it unto good,
to bring to pass, as it is this day, to save much people alive.
GENESIS 50:20

I do not need to remove the difficulty. It is no real problem to Me. It is only an anxiety manifesting itself in your mind and claiming the power to destroy.

I am restricted when you hold negative thoughts about the actions of other people. Release them to Me; otherwise you turn the action upon yourself to your own hurt.

from *Progress of Another Pilgrim*

THE ATTRIBUTE OF MERCY

Blessed are the merciful: for they shall obtain mercy.
MATTHEW 5:7

M ercy is one of My attributes which I strongly desire you to have.

Without this quality in ministry, there can be no genuine blessing flowing through your life.

Without mercy, Calvary would have become a preachment of condemnation rather than of forgiveness. Expressing His mercy toward His enemies, He provided you an example. You may never achieve an expression of love in the same degree, but let it be always the measure and the guide by which you judge your own attitudes.

from *Progress of Another Pilgrim*

365

ONE-MINUTE MEDITATIONS

April 16

WORDS OF HEALING

Let the word of Christ dwell in you richly in all wisdom.
COLOSSIANS 3:16

Speak evil of no man, but conceal the evil by speaking that which is good. (Love covers a multitude of sins, and it is the glory of love to conceal a matter.) In so doing you will heal, not wound. You desire to have a healing ministry. Let it embrace both the body and the soul, and be not content to heal bodies while wounding souls.

Learn to minister blessing and comfort to the spirit through your words and thus enhance the ministry of physical healing.

from *Progress of Another Pilgrim*

April 17

WHATSOEVER YOU SOW

I will give you rest.
MATTHEW 11:28

So long as there is disease in your thoughts, there will be disease in your body. Only when your mind is at rest can your body build health. Worry is an actively destructive force. Anxiety produces tension, and tension is the road to pain. Fear is devastating to the physical well-being of the body. Anger throws poison into the system that no antibiotic can ever counteract.

Whatsoever you sow in your secret thought-life, that shall you reap. Sow praise, and you shall reap joy and well-being and a strong faith.

from *Come Away My Beloved*

MY HOLY SPIRIT JUDGES

But if ye will not do so, behold, ye have sinned against the LORD:
and be sure your sin will find you out.
NUMBERS 32:23

*I*f you walk now in the light of My revealed truth and if you judge yourselves, you will not be judged at that coming day. And if you allow the searching eye of the Holy Spirit to find you out, then it will not be said to you, "Your sin will find you out." Do not resist Me or harden your hearts. Do not provoke Me to use My chastening rod, for I love you.

from *Come Away My Beloved*

FAITH RELEASED

Whosoever will save his life shall lose it: and whosoever
will lose his life for my sake shall find it.
MATTHEW 16:25

I will be your peace. Storms shall not disquiet the trusting heart, but songs of praise and victory shall spring from the place of testing, and mercy shall prevail where faith is released.

No harm can come to the one who looks to Me as his protection, but he who endeavors to protect himself shall be exposed to the destructive forces he seeks to escape.

He shall not know peace who runs after the rewards of the world.

from *On the Highroad of Surrender*

ONE-MINUTE MEDITATIONS
365

April 20

THE HEAVENLY QUEST

He is. . .a man of sorrows, and acquainted with grief.
ISAIAH 53:3

*M*any heartaches come to those who follow Me. Some are common to all men; others are the direct result of simply being a disciple of one who Himself was called "a Man of sorrows, and acquainted with grief" (Isaiah 53:3). If you are obedient to Me, you will experience a similar kind of suffering, the suffering of spiritual sacrifice. It is not self-sacrifice, it is the heavenly quest for total abandonment to the will of God.

from *Make Haste My Beloved*

April 21

VIVID RELATIONSHIP

Out of his mouth goeth a sharp sword, that with it he should smite the nations:
and he shall rule them with a rod of iron.
REVELATION 19:15

*B*lessed, holy sacrificial Lamb of God! What depth of love Thou hast demonstrated for us through Thy vicarious death on Calvary; and in Thy resurrection, what sublime victory! What dynamic power was revealed in Thine ascension, what promise of life to come, of ultimate triumph, of complete deliverance from this present world.

What great hope is set before us! What glory; what rapture—what a mighty deliverance—what victory! Christ has overcome.

from *Dialogues with God*

ANTICIPATION, MEDITATION, PARTICIPATION

He taught. . . . He healed. . . .
And in the morning. . .departed into a solitary place.
MARK 1:22, 34–35

*A*s you have honored Me with your lips, honor Me now with your ministry. Move on into active participation in My Will. Anticipation, meditation, and participation: there is a place for each of these as you move from one to the other.

Never get bogged down at any one of these points. Each is enriched by the other. In solitude I minister to you, and in service I minister through you. Both are essential.

from On the Highroad of Surrender

_____

_____

_____

_____

_____

GIVE ME THE FIRSTFRUITS

April 23

Keep the sabbath day to sanctify it, as the LORD thy God
hath commanded thee.
DEUTERONOMY 5:12

*G*ive Me a heart that has learned how to become quiet and to rest. Anybody can work. Few people know how to be quiet. Ye must be able to collect yourself—to take time to absorb the Spirit of God. For to be freshly filled with the Spirit will bring the guidance and direction and wisdom and the will to do His bidding.

from Dialogues with God

_____

_____

_____

_____

_____

THE NEED FOR GREATER FAITH

If any of you lack wisdom, let him ask of God.
JAMES 1:5

April 24

*D*o not expect the trials to be lighter than in the past. I test all things, and there are areas of your life that as yet I have not touched. Do not look for respite. The days ahead may call for greater endurance and more robust faith than you ever needed before.

Apply your heart to learn wisdom. This goal transcends every other aim, and any other good that comes out of a pressure period is an added blessing in excess.

Seek Me above all else.

from *Come Away My Beloved*

April 25

BE RESPONSIVE

But the LORD was not in the wind.
1 KINGS 19:11

*B*e responsive to the promptings of the Holy Spirit. I may not speak with a blast of the trumpet. It may be a touch on the shoulder. Do not wait for some climactic experience. Follow the still, small voice. Be obedient to the gentle moving of My Spirit. I often work this way because I want to develop your sensitivity.

I know your frailties, but in this way I purpose to make you strong. By working with you in this quiet fashion, I would strengthen your faith.

from *Progress of Another Pilgrim*

FAITH REACHES BEYOND

What things soever ye desire, when ye pray,
believe that ye receive them, and ye shall have them.
MARK 11:24

*F*aith reaches out beyond the need and into the supply, and always remember that the supply is greater than the need.

Do you need forgiveness? Lo, I have provided enough that if all human souls ever created turned to Me in repentance, they would be fully pardoned.

Do you need power to overcome temptation? Lo, I have overcome, and in Me there is victory.

It is patience for which you pray? That for which you wait is already given and only waits your receiving.

from On the Highroad of Surrender

PROTECTION

April 27

The LORD opened the eyes of the young man. . .and, behold,
the mountain was full of horses and chariots of fire round about Elisha.
2 KINGS 6:17

*M*y protection is all you need, My child. Gehazi owed his own safety to Elisha, for God was with Elisha, in the form of an angelic host that filled the mountains, and Gehazi, the servant, benefited by being in his company. So shall it be for those who journey with you, as God, seeing your confidence in Him and desire to please Him and do His will, moves in your behalf.

from On the Highroad of Surrender

April 28

GOOD AND EVIL

Walk worthy of the Lord.
COLOSSIANS 1:10

*E*very foot of ground where you tread, that will I give you. Walk in faith, and I will reward you with an abundance of fruit.

It is not in your heart to discern your own way. Much that is evil you call good, and much that is good you curse because you will bless what you enjoy and condemn what gives you displeasure.

I say unto you, My hand does not always deal joy. Fear not. I am not only wise but kind, and today's grief may become the channel for tomorrow's blessing.

from *On the Highroad of Surrender*

_____

_____

_____

_____

_____

April 29

I HAVE BUILT A HEDGE

Hast not thou made an hedge about him?
JOB 1:10

I have built a hedge about you, even as was written concerning Job. This was not a false accusation of the devil to Job: It was an actual reality. I only removed it to test and to prove him and to put to silence the enemy of his soul. But for multitudes of My children I have never removed the hedge. I am keeping you, My child, and for one purpose in particular— that you be able to accomplish the task committed to you. Therefore, give diligence to your mission.

from *Progress of Another Pilgrim*

_____

_____

_____

_____

_____

FIGHT DISCOURAGEMENT

Seek those things which are above.
COLOSSIANS 3:1

Turn not from the path of truth. Many testings shall beset you, but your God shall be your refuge.

Open wide your soul, and the Lord will fill it with His goodness. Your heart shall drink in His mercy and love; for His ear is attuned to your cry, and your desire toward Him shall be generously rewarded.

He knows your need and the depth of your searching. Only as you fight discouragement can you make room for Him to bless you in full measure as He desires to do.

from Progress of Another Pilgrim

MY WORDS CANNOT WAIT

May 1

He which hath begun a good work in you will perform it.
PHILIPPIANS 1:6

The hour is late, and the time for ministering is limited. Hasten to finish the work. Do that which is nearest at hand. I shall open a way for its fulfillment, so you need not hold back, wondering how the provisions will be supplied.

My words cannot wait; but you have held them as though you thought the future would wait. Up! Delay no more. Obey Me, and do so quickly. I will empower and I will make all things possible as you move in obedience.

from On the Highroad of Surrender

YOUR BODY, A LIVING SACRIFICE

Present your bodies a living sacrifice, holy, acceptable unto God.
ROMANS 12:1

May 2

*Y*ield Me your body as a living sacrifice,
   and do not be conformed to the things of the world,
     but be transformed by the renewal of your mind.
       Set your affections on things of the Spirit,
     and do not be in bondage to the desires of the flesh.
  For I have purchased you at great price.
Yes, you are My special possession and My treasure.

from *Come Away My Beloved*

_____

_____

_____

_____

_____

May 3

COME INTO THE SECRET CHAMBERS
OF COMMUNION

*Pray to thy Father which is in secret; and thy Father which
seeth in secret shall reward thee openly.*
MATTHEW 6:6

*O*My beloved, My heart longs after you. Do not grieve Me by your indifference. I would gather you; but you do not heed Me. I would embrace and caress you; but you are impatient to be on your way. You cannot please Me thus.

I have called you to come into the secret chambers of solitary communion. They are dark; but the comfort of My Person is there. Out of darkness comes great treasure.

from *Come Away My Beloved*

_____

_____

_____

_____

Repentance Activates My Grace

If we confess our sins, he is faithful and just to forgive us our sins,
and to cleanse us from all unrighteousness. If we say that we have not sinned,
we make him a liar, and his word is not in us.
1 John 1:9–10

*G*ive Me all: your body, mind, and spirit. Hold nothing back for yourself. Speak to Me often and much. The more you do so, the more I can help you. Full confession brings full forgiveness. True humility opens the door to divine aid. Genuine repentance activates My grace.

from *Progress of Another Pilgrim*

Chastening

Ye are the salt of the earth: but if the salt have lost his savour,
wherewith shall it be salted? it is thenceforth good for nothing.
Matthew 5:13

*H*ave I not said that unless you experience chastening, you may well doubt your sonship? Why then should you shrink from My rod of correction? You are not the parent, but the child.

Discipline and correction must come if you desire to be brought into conformity to My divine will. Accept My blessings and My comfort, but do not despise My stern dealings. All are working toward your ultimate perfection.

from *Come Away My Beloved*

May 6

TRIUMPHS RISE OUT OF DEFEATS

If we suffer, we shall also reign with him:
if we deny him, he also will deny us.
2 TIMOTHY 2:12

*B*e patient as My hand deals with you. Blessings are born out of pain. Triumphs rise out of the dust of defeats when the defeats are offered up to Me and you go on again in faith.
    Never despair.

from *Progress of Another Pilgrim*

_____

_____

_____

_____

_____

May 7

THE QUIET SPIRIT

Who shall ascend into the hill of the LORD?. . . He that hath clean hands,
and a pure heart; who hath not. . .sworn deceitfully.
PSALM 24:3–4

*B*e silent when you come to Me. Only the quiet spirit enters the place of communion. Strivings are left outside. Vexations bar the door, for they are caused by reactions to things, places, and people, and none of these are related to worship. Put them out of the temple. They that have clean hands and a pure heart shall ascend unto the mountain of the Lord.

from *On the Highroad of Surrender*

_____

_____

_____

_____

_____

GRACE

Then shall we know, if we follow on to know the LORD: his going forth is prepared as the morning; and he shall come unto us as the rain.
HOSEA 6:3

May 8

*F*ollow righteousness, and pursue it with unmitigated fervor. It is the only pursuit that is legitimate for the Christian. I have given My promise that I will supply every other need if you seek righteousness. It is in the selfless abandon to the Spirit that grace is nurtured.

I have freely extended My grace to you. Now I desire to see My grace developed in you!

from *Progress of Another Pilgrim*

_____

_____

_____

_____

_____

GIVE ME A DRINK

May 9

And Elijah said unto her, Fear not. . .but make me thereof a little cake first.
1 KINGS 17:13

*G*ive Me just a cupful of your limited affection. I will pour out upon you such love as you have never known. Love that will flood your whole being with such satisfaction as you never dreamed possible to experience except in Heaven. I beg of you, "Give Me a drink." Or in the language of Elijah, "Make me a small cake from it first" (1 Kings 17:13–16) and you will never lack for meal and oil.

from *Come Away My Beloved*

_____

_____

_____

_____

_____

ONE-MINUTE MEDITATIONS

May 10

END-TIME TENSIONS

Go out to battle: for God is gone forth before thee.
1 CHRONICLES 14:15

*M*y grace and mercy are intensified, not in spite of, but because of the tensions of the end-time. My love is moving in surrendered hearts.

Lift up your heads. For in the Spirit you shall listen and hear the sound of a great army readying for battle, and there shall be the sound of going in the tops of the mulberry trees, and they who have been enlisted by the Spirit shall go forth conquering and to conqueror.

from *On the Highroad of Surrender*

May 11

HARMONY WITH THE MESSAGE

I will run the way of thy commandments, when thou shalt enlarge my heart.
PSALM 119:32

I have many glorious things to reveal to you, but you must pay the price of treasuring, reverencing, and living in harmony with the message. Truth is always straightforward, and so also must be the one who receives it, or if he is not already, he must be willing to be made so.

I need your consent, your desire to be made holy. Surely I will answer when you call, and I will work in patience and in gentleness, but I will not stop until the perfecting process is finished.

from *On the Highroad of Surrender*

Find Solitude

Forty years didst thou sustain them in the wilderness,
so that they lacked nothing.
Nehemiah 9:21

I take no pleasure in the affliction of My children. In love I chasten to prevent the deeper suffering involved. But My heart is glad when you walk close, with your hand in Mine, and we may talk over the plans for each day's journey and activities so that it becomes a happy way that we travel in mutual fellowship.

So pour out your praise to Me from a light heart. I will plan your path and we will go singing.

from *Come Away My Beloved*

_____

_____

_____

_____

_____

I Require More

Yield yourselves unto God.
Romans 6:13

S trive to be perfectly yielded to the Holy Spirit. He will do much for you beyond what has been done in you up to this point. You have truly given Me much in the past, but I require more now because of the ministry I have for you to accomplish.

Let Me work in you with full liberty. You cannot do it yourself. I am the sanctifier. Only give Me the freedom to work. You will be amazed at how easily it can be done.

from *Progress of Another Pilgrim*

_____

_____

_____

_____

_____

ONE-MINUTE MEDITATIONS

May 14

TRIM YOUR WICK

Search me, O God, and know my heart. . .
and lead me in the way everlasting.
PSALM 139:23–24

*O*My child, do not that which I have not bidden. In My Name alone you ought to minister, and only when your own soul is free can the Spirit move unhindered.

Not only is time wasted when you disobey Me, but many souls are damaged, and your own no less.

Never try to evaluate a situation. Obey Me.

Trim your wick and polish your lamp. Your light is growing dim. Come back to listening only to My voice.

from *On the Highroad of Surrender*

May 15

THE CALL OF THE SPIRIT

Work out your own salvation with fear and trembling.
For it is God which worketh in you.
PHILIPPIANS 2:12–13

*T*oday is the day of salvation. Tomorrow is not given you to possess. Tomorrow is not a mysterious unknown: it will be the fruitage of what you sow today. Your response to Me at this moment becomes your present experience of salvation. Your answer to My call at the point where you now find yourself is the one deciding factor.

Regret weakens, and procrastination destroys the vision.

With a whole heart seek my face.

from *On the Highroad of Surrender*

TRUE PEACE AND FALSE

There is a way which seemeth right unto a man,
but the end thereof are the ways of death.
PROVERBS 14:12

*P*eace is in the full expression of My will. Anything short of this is a false peace, a sort of stupor that overtakes the one who is no longer spiritually sensitive. This is often mistaken for true peace in a way that can be compared to the freezing man who feels sleepy, not knowing he is slipping into the very jaws of death.

Make sure that your peace is the result of actively being in the will of God.

from *Progress of Another Pilgrim*

FIRST PLACE

May 17

Even Christ pleased not himself.
ROMANS 15:3

*E*very soldier must give first place to his obligation to the armed forces, and second place to his own private life and wishes. Even so you must do, if you would be My followers. Even so did Jesus during His earthly ministry. His entire life was subordinated to the Father's will.

Only that generated within you by the Spirit of God can bring forth righteousness; do not be conformed to this world, but be transformed by the renewing of your mind, that you may personally discover the perfect will of God.

from *Come Away My Beloved*

May 18

NOT LETHARGY BUT SURRENDER

He that doeth the will of God abideth for ever.
1 JOHN 2:17

*Y*ou are called not to lethargy but surrender.

Happy is the man who puts his trust in the Lord, yes, even to the extent that he lets Him formulate the plans and direct the goings.

No reward is sweeter than to feel His commendation. No life is more tranquil than that lived in His will. At His feet there is peace. Turmoil shall not dwell in the home where Christ is the honored guest.

Life becomes a hymn of praise when God's love rules the heart.

from *Progress of Another Pilgrim*

May 19

ANGELS ASSIST YOU

I will extol thee, O LORD; for thou hast lifted me up, and hast not made my foes to rejoice over me. . . .
I cried unto thee, and thou hast healed me.
PSALM 30:1–2

*O*My child, do not weep.

I am in the midst, and I am a strong deliverer. Courage is the greatest contribution you can make at this point. To be strong now will make the path of recovery easier.

Never underestimate the power of faith. Hold fast. Trust. Unseen angels assist you. Doors are opening to let you pass into safety.

from *On the Highroad of Surrender*

PRAYING IN THE SPIRIT

Praying in the Holy Ghost, keep yourselves in the love of God.
JUDE 20–21

*B*y praying in the
        Spirit,
        you will find your faith strengthened
        and your life bathed in My love.
With your faith laying hold on My promises and power,
        and your actions motivated by My love,
you will find yourself in the path of My activity.

from *Come Away My Beloved*

_____

_____

_____

_____

_____

THE PROPHET'S TONGUE

May 21

Let your speech be always with grace, seasoned with salt,
that ye may know how ye ought to answer every man.
COLOSSIANS 4:6

*N*o prophet of Mine is worthy of the name who brings reproach upon Zion by a careless
tongue. He who speaks My words at any time must guard his lips at all times. He is an
unworthy mouthpiece who delivers My message in one breath and denies Me in a selfish
moment by words that offend My Spirit.

from *Make Haste My Beloved*

_____

_____

_____

_____

_____

A SECRET PROCESS

Every maid's turn was come to go in to king Ahasuerus,
after that she had been twelve months.
ESTHER 2:12

I am perfecting inner beauty of the soul, as Esther was prepared to meet the king. I am doing a similar thing with My Church. My Bride is undergoing her beautification in anticipation of the coming of the Bridegroom.

I have ordained special ones to carry out this work of preparing the Bride. I commend you into their hands. Only so can you be presented before the King, purged of flaws and imperfections.

from *On the Highroad of Surrender*

May 23

LOVE ENDURES

He hath filled the hungry with good things;
and the rich he hath sent empty away.
LUKE 1:53

*T*he soul that submits to My disciplines loves Me. Love will hold you steady beneath the chastening rod because love believes and hopes in all things (1 Corinthians 13:7). Love will never fail. It will endure whatever comes because it rests in Me rather than in the circumstance.

You need never be deprived of comfort as long as your desires are fulfilled in Me; for I satisfy the hungry with good things, while the rich go empty away.

from *On the Highroad of Surrender*

THE GOLDEN PATH

The Lord God. . .revealeth his secret unto his servants.
AMOS 3:7

I have a special path for you. Search it out diligently. Let Me guide you in it. Follow not other sheep aimlessly as they roam through My pastures.

I have you on a path which is all your own. It is not My way for anybody else. It will become clear to you only by revelation from Me.

I call it the golden path. It is a sacred secret between us. Guard it and keep it, and treasure it in the secret places of your soul.

from *Progress of Another Pilgrim*

MY KINGDOM IS AT HAND

May 25

The hour of his judgment is come.
REVELATION 14:7

*B*y My Spirit, I will speak to My people. Those who hear My voice will sing of My glory. Those who are pure of heart will walk in a path of delight. Joy is the natural climate of heaven, and My chosen ones will have a full portion even now.

Be prepared for Me, for I will come to you in blinding splendor. Look above the present scene, for to dwell on the confusion of the world would render you unfit for the revelation of heaven.

from *Come Away My Beloved*

May 26

THE FEAR OF GOD

Thou shalt have no other gods before me.
EXODUS 20:3

*Y*es, My child, if you would search Me out, learn what it is to know the fear of God. Make of your heart a citadel of sacred worship, knowing that as you kneel at the altar of consecration, you shall receive of My grace and mercy and you shall behold mysterious things hidden from the carnal eye and withheld from the self-absorbed. For love of self will keep you from this place as surely as baser sins.

from *Make Haste My Beloved*

_____

_____

_____

_____

_____

May 27

REMOVE THE BARRIERS

All day long I have stretched forth my hands unto a disobedient and gainsaying people.
ROMANS 10:21

*M*y children, over many barriers I call to you.

I do not withhold Myself by choice, but you prevent Me from fellowshipping with you. Curtains of doubt, fear, timidity, unrepentance, and many others hide My face from you so that you cannot know Me.

Before it is too late, turn to Me with no devices of self-defense, and then can I open My heart to you and pour out My blessings.

from *On the Highroad of Surrender*

_____

_____

_____

_____

_____

VISION VERSUS DREAMS

I count all things but loss for the excellency of the knowledge of
Christ Jesus my Lord. . .that I may win Christ.
PHILIPPIANS 3:8

*M*y blessing should be of more value to you than all your possessions, and yes, even more than your aspirations and ideals, for these are still expressions of the desire of the ego for fulfillment.

In My Spirit there can be no cherishing of personal dreams. Only the doing of the Father's will is to be sought, and there is a vast difference between a God-inspired vision and personal dreams and aspirations.

from On the Highroad of Surrender

_____

_____

_____

_____

LOVE'S SERVANT

May 29

He that is greatest among you shall be your servant.
MATTHEW 23:11

*L*ove changes all the desires. Love knows that doing the Father's will is the only thing of value. Because love does not seek its own, it is not dismayed when circumstances are unfavorable.

He who has love will labor happily though unremunerated and sacrifice personal comfort without protest or complaint. He will measure happiness by his power to give and weakness by his limitation to bring comfort to those in need. Love is the source of joy, the touchstone of all meaningful human expression.

from Make Haste My Beloved

_____

_____

_____

_____

_____

May 30

THE HARVEST IS OVERRIPE

Put ye in the sickle, for the harvest is ripe.
JOEL 3:13

The hour is late. Be diligent. The harvest is overripe, and because it is so, there is need for greater care in the gathering of it. There is need for greater tenderness. . .for greater compassion. . .for infinite patience. This is a delicate work. When you deal with the souls of men, you are touching the most precious thing there is. Seek Me continually for direction and for understanding, so that you may be able to gather the overripe fruit without bruising it.

from *Progress of Another Pilgrim*

May 31

THE OIL OF CONSECRATION

*Thus shall they prepare. . .the oil, every morning
for a continual burnt offering.*
EZEKIEL 46:15

All your ministry must be blessed by the oil of consecration. Not one thing can be withheld. That which is most precious must be daily offered in dedication. Anything which is unworthy or evil must be given to Me so that it may be taken away; but the pure and good must be given to Me also, so that you may be continually freed from clasping it to yourself.

Anything you grasp becomes a burden. Give all to Me in a daily morning offering.

from *Progress of Another Pilgrim*

UNQUESTIONING TRUST

Trust in the LORD with all thine heart.
PROVERBS 3:5

*Y*ou need My blessing more than you need the help of all others combined. How often have I asked you to follow Me? I look to see you following, and instead I see you standing still and reckoning—or worse, fainting by the wayside.

It is your total commitment for which I wait. It is your unquestioning trust for which I yearn. It is your love flowing in utter simplicity which alone opens your channel to receive My mercies.

You can turn your burdens into blessings by giving Me everything.

from *Progress of Another Pilgrim*

NO SEPARATION

I saw a new heaven and a new earth.
REVELATION 21:1

*H*e has stretched forth His mighty hand
And has smitten the waters:
He has made me to pass through dry-shod. Hallelujah!
    For there will be no more sea.
There will be no more separation!
He has removed every barrier; He has bridged the gulf.
    He has drawn me unto Himself, yes, into Himself.

from *Come Away My Beloved*

June 3

PRESS ON

*I press toward the mark for the prize of the high calling
of God in Christ Jesus.*
PHILIPPIANS 3:14

*Y*ou have crossed a bridge. Reach not back. Move on ahead and press into the fullness of all I have prepared for you. It is waiting for you to step forward and receive. Do not tarry, and do not question, neither allow doubts to enter your mind. Your heart may cry out and rebel, but if you will turn to Me in those moments, I will give you My peace. I send you no place except as I have gone before.

from *On the Highroad of Surrender*

June 4

THE FATHER'S HOUSE

*One thing have I desired of the LORD, that will I seek after;
that I may dwell in the house of the LORD all the days of my life.*
PSALM 27:4

*I*n My Father's house are many mansions, and there is a place for you, My child. Look not for a place in the world. Your place is in the Father's house.

You are not of the world, even as I was not of the world. The spirit is nourished only by the eternal, and in prayer the soul breathes the atmosphere of heaven.

from *On the Highroad of Surrender*

PROVISION

My God shall supply all your need.
PHILIPPIANS 4:19

*M*y promises wait their fulfillment in the lives of My children. So much I would give, so little is received. Why live so beggarly when the riches of heaven are yours for the asking? Having learned to receive from Me, you will find it easy to give to all others, for you shall have no fear of lack, and no need to guard your supply. Having found the source, you shall never want.

Walk in the freedom of My abundance, looking to Me for all things.

from On the Highroad of Surrender

HEAVEN IS YOUR PORTION

Thou wilt shew me the path of life: in thy presence is fulness of joy;
at thy right hand there are pleasures for evermore.
PSALM 16:11

*O*nly the courageous discover My riches. Faintheart will content himself with what his eye beholds. The Spirit in you is wiser and will gladly fling aside all material blessings to lay hold on eternal life. The Spirit is not enticed by the glitter of gold nor tempted to desert heavenly vision in favor of temporal blessings.

from Make Haste My Beloved

June 7

THE IMPORTANCE OF TIME AND KINDNESS

Walk in love, as Christ also hath loved us.
EPHESIANS 5:2

*T*ime is of supreme importance. Let Me help you know what is worthy of attention and what is not; otherwise you may be tempted to eliminate the things I most desire you to do.

Having a schedule will help you, but remember that kindness is more indicative of spiritual fervor than all your efficiency in work. Never let your works of righteousness crowd out the little acts of thoughtfulness. The labors of the hands must never take precedence over the gentle expressions of a compassionate heart.

from *Progress of Another Pilgrim*

June 8

A YIELDED SPIRIT

Obey the voice of the LORD thy God.
DEUTERONOMY 27:10

*U*nless you move in obedience, all your other actions and your knowledge will be misdirected and unfruitful. Know My will, and do it. I have revealed it to you and I am constantly seeking to guide you in myriad ways. Your self-will blots out My divine directives. Before the sound of My voice registers on your consciousness, you drown it out with the objections of an unyielded spirit. You will never move freely in My highest purpose unless you constantly offer up to Me a yielded, broken, self-renouncing vessel.

from *On the Highroad of Surrender*

PREPARATION

Study to shew thyself approved unto God. . .
rightly dividing the word of truth.
2 TIMOTHY 2:15

*M*y child, I would speak to you as to a disciple. What is in your hand? Would you attempt to do a work with a broken instrument? You desire to serve Me in many ways. Have you carefully prepared? Or do you expect Me to overrule your lack of wisdom? Lo, I say unto you, preparation is your own responsibility. Certainly I will help you in it, but I am not glorified through a vessel that is careless concerning its condition.

from *Progress of Another Pilgrim*

IDENTITY

If a man say, I love God, and hateth his brother. . .whom he hath seen,
how can he love God whom he hath not seen?
1 JOHN 4:20

I am shaping you in the furnace of affliction that I may set My seal upon you and display in you My own identity. I desire that you be one with Me in all I have purposed.

My heart is grieved when those who profess to be My children neglect their intercessory prayer life. Can you love God while ignoring the need of your brother?

from *On the Highroad of Surrender*

June 11

SPEAK THE WORD OF FAITH

Pray ye therefore the Lord of the harvest, that he would send forth labourers into his harvest.
LUKE 10:2

*L*earn to speak the word of faith and knowledge as I put it in your mouth. Doors will be opened in this simple fashion, and entrance given to hearts that would otherwise have remained closed to the gospel. Once the door is open, you may plant the seed of faith and it will spring forth into eternal life.

Go to the tender, the needy, the brokenhearted, and the suffering. I shall minister in love and compassion, and I shall use you as My mouthpiece.

from *On the Highroad of Surrender*

June 12

THE SEEDS OF THE WORD

Here am I; send me.
ISAIAH 6:8

*L*o, the message is Mine, but I have need of those who will speak it without alteration and without any attempt to please men.

The seeds of the Word have long since dried up and died in many a prayerless life. I need those who will speak it again and send it out afresh in the dynamic power of the Holy Spirit. The Word must be spoken through those who are spiritually alive, otherwise it loses its power to produce new life.

from *Progress of Another Pilgrim*

AN ANOINTED TONGUE

The LORD. . .sent them two and two before his face into every city and place, whither he himself would come.
LUKE 10:1

I have called you to a special ministry, and it cannot be carried out properly without My full blessing.

Let Me anoint your tongue, and you shall speak with divine authority and never again will you say, "I am a weak and inadequate vessel." I shall put words into your heart and speak them forth from your lips, and hearts shall burn as the message goes out.

from *Progress of Another Pilgrim*

IMMEDIATE OBEDIENCE

If ye be willing and obedient, ye shall eat the good of the land.
ISAIAH 1:19

W hen I give you guidance and you are persuaded in your own mind of My leading, never ponder your decision. There is but one possible reply, and that is "Yes, Lord." Then simply do My bidding, and do it immediately.

Delayed obedience is nearly always disobedience, because along with the procrastination there is deliberation followed by rationalization, and by the time decision finally evolves into action, your own will is in control.

from *On the Highroad of Surrender*

365
ONE-MINUTE MEDITATIONS

June 15

BE MY ALLY

Come ye yourselves apart. . .and rest a while.
MARK 6:31

*D*o not fear nor resist My voice. When I speak to you, you will know that it is I, the Lord God. As I spoke to Isaiah I will speak to you.

Your busyness wearies Me. Your fretfulness grieves Me. I long to take it from you and give you instead the balm of Gilead. Be My ally. I will endow you with life so dynamic that you will serve Me before you have time to even think about putting forth the effort to do so.

from Come Away My Beloved

_____

_____

_____

_____

_____

June 16

PERSPECTIVE AND DEPTH

Teach me good judgment and knowledge.
PSALM 119:66

*Y*ou need perspective and depth. This never comes from public converse, but from private communion. You seek to learn from others, but I long to tell you things I may never be able to tell them. There are truths I wish to give you. You may never be asked to share them with any other person. They may be just for you—or they may be for people you have never seen as yet.

from Progress of Another Pilgrim

_____

_____

_____

_____

_____

BY SILENCE YE ROB ME OF MY GLORY

Whosoever. . .shall be ashamed of me and of my words. . .
of him also shall the Son of man be ashamed.
MARK 8:38

*B*y words a man may sin against Me, but by silence do ye rob
Me of My Glory.
And know this: as ye testify of Me
before men,
I will surely plead thy cause.
But if you are ashamed of Me before men, I will be ashamed of you
before the Father.

from *Dialogues with God*

PREPARE YOUR GARMENTS

She should be arrayed in fine linen, clean and white:
for the fine linen is the righteousness of saints.
REVELATION 19:8

*T*he day is at hand, and the Day Star riseth even now. You may not see Me yet, but I am only just beneath the rim of the horizon, and you shall behold Me shortly in all My glory.
How ought you to rise and make yourself ready! How you should put your house in order and prepare your garments!
Your garments shall be of fine linen, for it is the righteousness of the saints.

from *Progress of Another Pilgrim*

June 19

FRESH ANOINTING

He that doeth the will of God abideth for ever.
1 JOHN 2:17

Service to Me by the will of the flesh is temporal,
   but the doing of the will of God is eternal.
And this is the will of God, that ye be about the Father's business—
   that ye work the works of Him that hath called thee.
Leave all else to Me.
Seek the fresh anointing
            and I will do the rest.

from *Dialogues with God*

June 20

NEW SONGS IN YOUR MOUTH

*Unto you that fear my name shall the Sun of righteousness
arise with healing in his wings.*
MALACHI 4:2

O my soul, wait upon God, and He will do you good.
   Yes, He will refresh your soul.
For His tender mercies are never failing,
   and His kindness toward you is as the morning.
As the Sun of Righteousness shall arise
   with healing in His wings (see Malachi 4:2),
   so shall your God be unto you.

from *Come Away My Beloved*

Be Much with Me

Be ye therefore ready also: for the Son of man cometh
at an hour when ye think not.
LUKE 12:40

Set the watch in the nighttime; yes, rise and pray, and do not let that hour come upon you unaware.

For the time is short; yes, the storm is gathering fast. Can you not discern the events that are currently shaping up in the affairs of men, and be as keen to observe their portent?

Let My Spirit pervade your spirit, and you shall be more influenced by Me than by the world around you.

Be much with Me.

from *Come Away My Beloved*

Why Do You Falter?

I will go before thee, and make the crooked places straight.
ISAIAH 45:2

O My child, I have need of you. Have I not called you and blessed you? Have I not laid My hand upon you and shaped you for My purposes? Why, then, do you doubt?

I have tested your faith many times, and I know it is strong. Why do you falter? Rise, and go in My Name, knowing it is I who thrust you forth. It is not man. This is My plan for you. The way should be easy when you know this.

from *Progress of Another Pilgrim*

June 23

IONOSPHERIC CHRISTIAN LIVING

Stand fast therefore in the liberty wherewith Christ hath made us free.
GALATIANS 5:1

Stay in the flexibility of the Spirit. Live in the faith realm, and let your thoughts soar freely in the open skies of faith, where the things not yet seen become real to you. Call it ionospheric Christian living, if you wish. It will free you from bondages to people. It will not give you an independent nor rebellious feeling toward others, but will liberate you so that you will no longer feel the need to struggle against these hindrances.

from *Progress of Another Pilgrim*

June 24

TRUST

In God have I put my trust: I will not be afraid what man can do unto me.
PSALM 56:11

You struggle, My child, when you could as easily rest in My arms. You concern yourself with the actions of others and neglect the only important thing: to abide in Me. He who abides in me has no need to be anxious.

When you are moving out of My divine will, you have unrest. Abiding brings confiding, for to know Me is to trust Me, and trust brings peace.

from *On the Highroad of Surrender*

As a Lamb Before a Lion

Your adversary the devil, as a roaring lion, walketh about,
seeking whom he may devour.
I PETER 5:8

*A*ll kinds of dangers lurk about you. The enemy would rob you of the most sacred blessing. He has no desire to take it except to destroy it. Your power to protect it is no match for his treachery. He lies in wait in the unexpected place, and you are as a lamb before a lion.

At My feet leave all, and know it is for your ultimate joy. Truly it is not a sacrifice. It will be your salvation.

from *Progress of Another Pilgrim*

_____

_____

_____

_____

_____

Learn to Listen

He that refraineth his lips is wise.
PROVERBS 10:19

*W*hen you pray, My child, do not make it a one-way conversation. Know I am listening, but know also I will respond and will speak to you if you give Me opportunity. Prayer is not only of the lips, but of the ear also, for prayer is of the heart, and the heart that has learned to love has learned to listen more than to speak!

When you come to Me in prayer, you ought to come to enjoy Me, not to entertain Me.

from *On the Highroad of Surrender*

_____

_____

_____

_____

_____

COMMUNICATION

Our conversation is in heaven; from whence also we look for the Saviour.
PHILIPPIANS 3:20

June 27

Keep in vital communication with Me. Loose yourself from the world at every possible point. You can fulfill My purpose only when your channel is completely open and free to Me. Resist every hindrance. Yield to Me the deepest place in your consciousness. Only in this way do I have full control of your life energies. I will preserve them for the Spirit's activity as you abide in the place of communion.

Do not look for any other secret of spiritual power. There is none.

from *Progress of Another Pilgrim*

_____

_____

_____

_____

June 28

LEARN WELL AND LISTEN CLOSELY

Thou wilt keep him in perfect peace, whose mind is stayed on thee:
because he trusteth in thee.
ISAIAH 26:3

No disturbance, either in yourself or in others, can interfere with the moving of My Spirit if you do not focus attention upon it.

Be as a babe in its mother's arms and know that I carry you near to My heart, and this is why you have knowledge of many things not revealed to others. They must find this place for themselves before they can hear My voice. Meanwhile, you are My ambassador to them.

Learn well, and listen closely.

from *Progress of Another Pilgrim*

_____

_____

_____

_____

_____

Loose the Child

Cast thy burden upon the Lord, and he shall sustain thee.
PSALM 55:22

The little ones are in My care; you shall not be anxious. Rely on Me, for the tenderness of My love exceeds that of a mother.

Picture the Lord Jesus as He took the young children upon His knee. Trustingly place your child in His hands. They are healing hands, and you may count on Him to bring wholeness and perfection, whether here or in the Father's house.

Your heart is bound to the heart of the child. Loose the cord of affection lest it break.

from On the Highroad of Surrender

The Armour of Light

The way of man is not in himself: it is not in man that walketh to direct his steps.
JEREMIAH 10:23

No problem confronts you that I cannot resolve. Confess, and I will forgive, and I will extricate you from this situation.

I will go with you Myself and make the crooked places straight and we will go on again, together. This time you will wait for My leading.

Wear the armour of the Spirit, and you have My protection. Fear not what others can do to harm you. Fear only your own tendency to act independently.

from Progress of Another Pilgrim

ONE-MINUTE MEDITATIONS

THE CENTRIFUGAL POWER OF THE HOLY SPIRIT

Walk not after the flesh, but after the Spirit.
ROMANS 8:4

*A*ll kinds of contrivances will seek to throw you off balance. The centrifugal power of the Holy Spirit within you is ever seeking to draw you and keep you in the perfect divine pattern and form. Do not resist it. Rather, resist the pull of the external forces. It is the world, the flesh, and the devil which influence toward destruction and ugliness.

Only the divine Spirit of God—nothing else—can preserve your soul and life in the beauty of purity and the expression of grace.

from *Progress of Another Pilgrim*

July 1

July 2

THE DISCIPLINES OF FREEDOM

Stand fast therefore in the liberty wherewith Christ hath made us free,
and be not entangled again with the yoke of bondage.
GALATIANS 5:1

*O*My people, I bring you out of bondage as rapidly as you are able to cope with freedom. Hold fast in the liberty wherein I have set you free and allow not anyone to bring you back into subjection.

All sin is binding. In Christ is freedom, because in Him is holiness. The world with its desires passes away, but he who chooses to do the will of God will live forever.

from *On the Highroad of Surrender*

THE ECONOMY OF THE KINGDOM

With the same measure that ye mete withal
it shall be measured to you again.
LUKE 6:38

July 3

*B*ring Me all the tithes, and I will open the gates of heaven and pour down upon you a fourfold blessing. Yes, I will bless you in the grace of giving, and I will bless you with joy. You shall open the door of ministry for My servants, and you shall partake of the fruits that will come as a result.

You will never give to Me and become the poorer for it. In exchange for your small gifts, you shall be given My boundless riches.

from *Come Away My Beloved*

BE NOT NEGLIGENT

July 4

Stir up the gift of God, which is in thee.
2 TIMOTHY 1:6

*B*e not negligent concerning the gift I have given you. Do not allow it to become dormant. Be up and about your Father's business. Let nothing else claim priority over this.

You shall suffer loss, and not you alone but multitudes of others, if indolence overtakes you. My people are searching for food, and the pastures are sparse. There is need for the provision of nourishment. Yes, My Body must be fed and cared for and supplied the necessary nutriments for health and growth.

from *Progress of Another Pilgrim*

July 5

I MUST HAVE OVERCOMERS

The life which I now live. . .I live by the faith of the Son of God.
ROMANS 2:20

*Y*ou have faith in Me but faith without works is dead.

I must have overcomers through whom I may overcome. There is an enemy to be contested and defeated. My new life will become yours in direct proportion to your success in emptying your heart of self-will.

I know you cannot do this for yourself; but you must will it to be done. And as you will it, I will work with you and within you to bring it to pass.

from *Come Away My Beloved*

July 6

YOU ARE VIOLATING MY WILL

We then that are strong ought to bear the infirmities of the weak,
and not to please ourselves.
ROMANS 15:1

*M*y child, you are not where I would have you be. How can I be pleased with you? "Love," it is written, "seeketh not her own." But you have been pursuing your own ends, and this to Me is folly. What you desire may be beautiful and good and may constitute nothing that is harmful in itself; all the same, you are violating My will and marring My pattern.

from *Progress of Another Pilgrim*

AN UNCOMPLAINING HEART

Behold, happy is the man whom God correcteth...
he woundeth, and his hands make whole.
JOB 5:17–18

*B*ear joyfully My rod of correction. Know that while I minister to you, you are being prepared to minister to others. Make no mistake, there cannot be one without the other. Your attitudes need the disciplining of the Holy Spirit.

Rest in Me in the quiet place and give Me an uncomplaining heart. I will fill it with My Grace. When I see that you are ready to do it, I will make My will inescapable.

from On the Highroad of Surrender

BREAD UPON THE WATERS

Cast thy bread upon the waters: for thou shalt find it after many days.
ECCLESIASTES 11:1

*D*o not be afraid to follow Me, nor draw back in doubt. I will provide all that you lack, and I will pave the way for you with My bounty.

You will rejoice with exceeding joy, and your joy shall be shared by angels. They walk beside you and guard your way.

Never limit Me. I will take you through, though cliffs should rise before you. There will always be a provision, and in My mercy I will see that you find it.

from Come Away My Beloved

TRIBULATION

Beloved, think it not strange concerning the fiery trial which is to try you,
as though some strange thing happened unto you.
1 PETER 4:12

July 9

Through much tribulation I am bringing My chosen to perfection. Be not amazed when challenges present themselves. I am building your fortitude, and the day will come when you will be grateful for every lesson learned in the school of affliction.

from *On the Highroad of Surrender*

July 10

ETERNAL DESTINY OF THE PRESENT MOMENT

Be thou an example of the believers.
1 TIMOTHY 4:12

It is not appointed to you to know the future. It is enough that we should walk together in love and trust. No doubts need mar your peace. Rest in the knowledge that My ways are perfect and My grace is all-sufficient. My help is adequate, no matter what may befall you.

Live in the awareness of the eternal destiny of the present moment. To be unduly occupied with matters of the future is to your own disadvantage. So much is waiting to be done now.

from *Come Away My Beloved*

I Shall Gather My People

The time is come that judgment must begin at the house of God.
1 PETER 4:17

*T*oday is the day of salvation (see 2 Corinthians 6:2), and again: "Seek ye the LORD while He may be found" (Isaiah 55:6), for the night comes.

Lift your eyes to the clouds, for the heavens are filled with glory. Yes, He comes with ten thousand of His saints. Lift your hearts, for you will not be afraid of those things that are coming to pass upon the earth. For I shall gather My people to Myself; and the flames will not touch them.

from *Come Away My Beloved*

Maintain Constancy

July 12

For he satisfieth the longing soul, and filleth the hungry soul with goodness.
PSALM 107:9

*D*o not grieve, My child. You have need of nothing. Hold Me close to your heart, and I will satisfy every longing. Allow Me to comfort you, and you will find yourself reaching out less and less to others for support and solace.

Maintain a constancy in devotion, and I will be pleased and will do all manner of wonderful things in your behalf. I will cause blessings to be heaped upon you. You will be increased abundantly in the riches of the Kingdom.

from *On the Highroad of Surrender*

July 13

ETERNAL VALUES

For the which cause I also suffer these things: nevertheless I am not ashamed: for I know whom I have believed, and am persuaded that he is able to keep that which I have committed unto him against that day.

2 TIMOTHY 1:12

*E*very motion in your life becomes impregnated with sublime significance as you are wholly dedicated to Me. All of time becomes charged with eternal values as it is consecrated and given to Me.

from *Progress of Another Pilgrim*

July 14

TRUE DEDICATION

Search me, O God, and know my heart.
PSALM 139:23

I am calling you aside into a walk of Faith. There is no self-denial possible without full surrender. There are forms of self-punishment that cloak themselves in the robes of dedication but are really false expressions and not true piety. Only I can lay upon you a true spirit of humility and dedication. Only My love can motivate a genuine self-sacrifice.

Do not deceive yourself. Let Me try your motives and probe the depths of your heart. My intention is to bless you, not to cause you unnecessary suffering.

from *Progress of Another Pilgrim*

THE SPIRIT OF LIFE

Greater works than these shall he do.
JOHN 14:12

*M*y Spirit is the Spirit of Life, and I am in thee and upon thee that thou shouldst not be barren nor unfruitful;

and whomsoever thou touchest in faith shall feel My quickening power.

Life shall rise out of death; yea, Eternal Life out of spiritual death. Is this not even greater than My servant Lazarus?

For I said, "Greater works than I do shall ye do, because I go unto my Father."

from Dialogues with God

WITHDRAW YOUR FOOT

Where there is no talebearer, the strife ceaseth.
PROVERBS 26:20

*R*obbed of privacy, friendship is destroyed. There is a degree of reserve to which each soul has birthright, and which if relinquished to the curiosity of the impudent, leaves him stripped of the riches of his soul and robbed of his self-respect.

The riches of friendship are placed in the hands of those who prove themselves trustworthy. The ignorant will rob a nest of its eggs. The wise wait patiently for the sound of baby birds. He who steals the eggs deprives himself of this pleasure.

from On the Highroad of Surrender

July 17

SINCERITY

Be sober, be vigilant.
1 PETER 5:8

O My child, be truly as a little child, and preserve within your spirit the grace of simplicity. Maintain a candid honesty. Resist all temptation to put on airs. Be natural. Strive to be as Jesus, who was never pretentious, never evasive nor coy. Be real, be sincere, for to serve God demands sincerity. The needs of hearts and problems of life are real. Many carry burdens and griefs, and how can you be of help in a frivolous state of mind?

from *Progress of Another Pilgrim*

July 18

No Compromise!

Come out from among them, and be ye separate.
2 CORINTHIANS 6:17

There are ways to witness without compromising, but there is no way to compromise and at the same time effectively witness. "Come out from among them, and be separate." Those who seek the light will be drawn out into the light. Those who remain in the darkness do so because they prefer the darkness and to go back into darkness yourself, hoping to save them, will result in giving the evil one the opportunity to assail your own soul.

You cannot have both—light and darkness.

from *On the Highroad of Surrender*

Pride

The flesh lusteth against the Spirit, and the Spirit against the flesh.
GALATIANS 5:17

Stand firm in your convictions against the contrary wind. Every soul struggles against the elements. Thoughts of others can come upon you like a storm at sea until your boat is well-near swamped. Except for My grace, it would be destroyed. But I am near at hand. Purify your heart so that I can be glorified in all your thoughts and actions.

I am concerned for your victory. You may have it as you fall back into My arms and cease struggling.

from On the Highroad of Surrender

THE HEALING POOL

July 20

An angel went down. . .into the pool, and troubled the water: whosoever then first. . .stepped in was made whole.
JOHN 5:4

Whenever you are in any kind of trouble, know that My Spirit in the midst is like the angel who stirred the Pool of Bethesda and made it a place of healing. Disturbances which give every appearance of being natural become infused with divine purposes if your soul is allowed to lie in My hand.

I Myself touch circumstances and add the power of the miraculous.

from Progress of Another Pilgrim

July 21

COMFORT IN AFFLICTION

Seek my face: in their affliction they will seek me early.
HOSEA 5:15

*H*as not My hand fashioned for you many signs and wonders? Have I not ministered to you in miraculous ways? Will you not, then, trust Me now in this new emergency, even as you have trusted Me in the past?

Lean hard upon Me, for I bring you through to new victories, and restoration shall follow what seems now to be a wind of destruction. Draw upon the resources of My grace. Heaven rejoices when you go through trials with a singing spirit.

from *Come Away My Beloved*

July 22

CONCENTRATION

For we wrestle not against flesh and blood, but against principalities,
against powers, against the rulers of the darkness of this world,
against spiritual wickedness in high places.
EPHESIANS 6:12

*G*ive your full strength to the conflict. Think of nothing else. Only concentration brings results. Lo, the enemy is concentrating against you to destroy you.

Gird on your armor, for the battle is not against flesh and blood, but against principalities and powers and against spiritual forces of darkness intruding into sacred places. I am at your side to help you.

from *On the Highroad of Surrender*

THY GOD FOREVER

But the very hairs of your head are all numbered.
MATTHEW 10:30

*B*ehold, I am Thy God forever. I am with thee. In the time of trouble, I will be thy strong defense, and in the hour of need, I am thy sure habitation.

Mine eye is ever watchful and I shall undertake for thee according to My glorious riches. Is it not written: "the very hairs of your head are all numbered"? Surely My love for thee is altered by no external circumstances.

My love is constant. Hold to this one thing as the needle holds to the pole.

from Dialogues with God

RIVERS OF LIVING WATER

July 24

When the poor and needy seek water. . .I the LORD will hear them. . . .
I will open rivers in high places, and fountains in the midst of the valleys.
ISAIAH 41:17–18

*I*n the moment that you lift your voice to cry out to Me, then shall My glory gather you up. Yes, I shall wrap you in the garments of joy, and My presence shall be your great reward.

Lift your eyes to Mine. Lift your voice to Me in praise; in this way a fountain shall be opened within you, and you will drink of its refreshing waters.

from Come Away My Beloved

THE SPIRITUAL SENSES

The manifestation of the Spirit is given to every man to profit withal.
I CORINTHIANS 12:7

I will surely fill your vessel with a mighty downpour of My reviving Spirit. I will quicken your senses and you shall hear, speak, and discern in the Spirit. You shall verily feel in the same way. For as man has five natural senses, regenerated souls have five spiritual senses, and every alert, healthy believer should have these operating.

The power is given you already. Exercise it and let Me educate you along these lines.

from *Progress of Another Pilgrim*

July 26

BREAK OLD PATTERNS

Jesus said unto him, Follow me; and let the dead bury their dead.
MATTHEW 8:22

*T*he time is now. Run after Me as I move, because I am moving rapidly and am doing a quick work. Pay no attention to any voice except the voice of the Spirit. Let no one use you except the Father. Believe no one except the Son. Live in expectancy and move in absolute obedience.

Break out of old patterns, and make no provision for your own personal wishes. Purify your desires so that you do not stand in your own way.

from *Progress of Another Pilgrim*

USELESS STRIVING

The servant of the Lord must not strive.
2 TIMOTHY 2:24

*B*e careful that you are following Me, and I will care for all else. Striving is for those who have not yet learned to trust Me. Anxiety is the affliction of the self-possessed. The godly know their heritage and revel in the protection of their Redeemer. For it is in the blood of Jesus that refuge is found for every onslaught of the enemy.

from *Make Haste My Beloved*

CONVICTION AND FORGIVENESS

July 28

The effectual fervent prayer of a righteous man availeth much.
JAMES 5:16

*M*y patience is running out. I have willed and you have resisted me.

You are indulgent when I have called you to rigid discipline. You speak soft words when I would require you to speak the truth. You interfere with the convicting work of My Holy Spirit when you smooth over confession. I am not a severe God, unmindful of the frailties of human nature; but I am a God of divine love and holiness, and I desire your fellowship, and I long for you to know My joy.

from *Come Away My Beloved*

LET HIM TAKE THE INITIATIVE

Submit yourselves therefore to God.
JAMES 4:7

*L*et no selfish motives rule your actions. Be motivated by the love of God, and if you truly are, you can rest assured that whatever you do has the approval of your Father.

You cannot do with joy some of the things that may be permissible for another. You are not free to make your own choices as long as you are surrendered to the Will of God, for when you are yielded to Him, it is He who gives the directions. Wait for Him to take the initiative.

from *Progress of Another Pilgrim*

July 30

THE ART OF CONSTANCY

Praise. . .God continually.
HEBREWS 13:15

*I*n the midst of every legitimate activity your soul can be focused on Me if gratitude and adoration and worship have captured your heart. The soul of a man may be a continual chapel of praise as you learn the art of constancy in loving Me first and foremost.

You frequently emphasize how much you should love Me. But even more important is the constancy of your love, that it be the overflowing grace of your heart continually, so that every waking hour you are truly and literally walking and worshipping in the Spirit.

from *Progress of Another Pilgrim*

COURAGE

Take the helmet of salvation, and the sword of the Spirit.
EPHESIANS 6:17

*M*y people shall not go mourning, for I the Lord will be their rejoicing and their song. They will not be a complaining people, for I will take away the murmuring from your streets. I shall give My people brave and courageous spirits, and I will make them strong of heart. I will give them the spirit of the martyrs, for they will be My witnesses of resurrection power. They shall be stalwart. They shall be steadfast.

So take upon you the full armor of God.

from Come Away My Beloved

_____

_____

_____

_____

_____

FLEE COMPROMISE

August 1

We are more than conquerors through him that loved us.
ROMANS 8:37

*G*ird on the armor of truth and righteousness, and know that the battle is in full array. Not by might nor by power, but by My Spirit shall you be victorious, so do not seek to outwit the enemy by fleshly strategy. Only in the strength of the Lord shall you stand.

Flee compromise, for it leads always to defeat. The shed blood of Christ is your only protection. When you go into battle, go in My Name, and know that you go against an already-defeated foe.

from On the Highroad of Surrender

_____

_____

_____

_____

_____

I WILL BRING THE VICTORY

Thanks be to God, which giveth us the victory through our Lord Jesus Christ.
1 CORINTHIANS 15:57

August 2

*O*My child, have I ever failed you? Have I not been your refuge and your strong defense? Fear not. My purposes will be fulfilled in spite of your weaknesses, if in your need you rely on My strength.

I glory in overruling the prevailing circumstances, and I take pleasure in bringing victories in those places where no victory is anywhere in sight.

Count on My coming.

Ask for the victory. I will come and bring it.

from *Come Away My Beloved*

August 3

ANXIETY

Rejoicing in hope; patient in tribulation; continuing instant in prayer.
ROMANS 12:12

*M*y child, when you are tired, do not be disheartened. Most of your discouragement comes when you carry your own burden, forgetting to call upon Me for help. Give Me everything, and quickly; for as soon as any heaviness of spirit sets in, trust is crowded out. An atmosphere of anxiety or unhappiness is withering to faith.

Continual prayer will fortify your soul.

from *On the Highroad of Surrender*

LEARN TO REIGN

We are more than conquerors through him that loved us.
ROMANS 8:37

*Y*ou are more than conquerors.

Rise up, then, and lay claim to the power that is yours, because I am in you, and you are in Me, and as I was in the world, so are you I was victorious, and you too may be victorious. I withstood every encounter with the devil, and you too can stand against him. I healed the sick and wrested tortured bodies out of the grip of evil forces, and you too can do the same.

Learn to reign, for I have made you to become kings and priests.

from *Come Away My Beloved*

DISCOVER THE POWER OF TRUTH

*For the word of God is quick, and powerful,
and sharper than any twoedged sword.*
HEBREWS 4:12

*D*iscover the power of Truth—any truth. Put it to the test. Every truth is as firm as I am. It can be relied upon. It can be trusted as a fact and counted upon in experience.

Believe My truths, but go beyond this. Put them into operation, and learn what it is to experience them as well. Only in this way can you proclaim their fact in a persuasive manner. No teaching is effective except as it springs out of experience.

from *Progress of Another Pilgrim*

WISDOM, A GIFT

He that goeth about as a talebearer revealeth secrets:
therefore meddle not with him that flattereth with his lips.
PROVERBS 20:19

*M*uch false doctrine has been generated out of man's fleshly desire to possess knowledge not yet revealed. In his impertinence, he has resented even the silence of God and expressed his intolerance of this silence by fabricating ideas of his own.

Information wrongly acquired or inaccurately interpreted becomes a curse rather than a blessing. Be content to know only what is freely revealed by either God or man, and be not a scavenger of worthless information.

from *On the Highroad of Surrender*

THE LISTENING EAR

Take heed what ye hear: with what measure ye mete,
it shall be measured to you: and unto you that hear shall more be given.
MARK 4:24

I will make My message very clear to the honest heart. You would be furthered more in your spiritual life if you spent more time praying that duplicity be eradicated from your heart than by praying to have more truth revealed to you. In most cases, you already have knowledge of more truth than you are practicing. To seek further truth before surrendering to the light already received is to invite destruction.

from *On the Highroad of Surrender*

THE BROADENING VIEW

For there is nothing hid, which shall not be manifested.
MARK 4:22

*G*ive yourself to diligent study—yea, search the Scriptures for they are given for the purpose of revealing Me. It shall be as when one ascends a mountain, and from each successively higher vantage point he thrills at an increasingly broadening view. I will take you progressively higher via the written Word until that day when you shall see Me face-to-face! Then shall you know Me and understand Me even as I now know you.

from *Dialogues with God*

THE LANGUAGE OF LOVE

Keep thy heart with all diligence; for out of it are the issues of life.
PROVERBS 4:23

*B*e silent, My child, and when you speak, let it be your heart that calls My name. Many have My name upon their lips but their hearts are a hollow shell. Love is not in a mouth that is full, but in an overflowing heart.

I listen for the words of your heart. I understand the language of love.

When you listen for My voice, listen with your heart.

from *On the Highroad of Surrender*

Be Thou My Door of Hope

It is of the Lord's mercies that we are not consumed, because his compassions fail not.
They are new every morning: great is thy faithfulness.
LAMENTATIONS 3:22–23

*O*ut of the depths you have cried unto Me. I am gracious and full of compassion. My heart is touched by the feeling of your infirmities, and I am acquainted with your grief (Hebrews 4:15).

I am your help, for to whom else shall you go? I will be your Door of Hope, though darkness is round about you.

from *On the Highroad of Surrender*

August 11

A Beautiful Work

He is a chosen vessel unto me, to bear my name.
ACTS 9:15

*Y*ou are Mine. You are not your own. With a great price I have purchased you for Myself. If you will listen to Me, I will reveal to you more fully so that you may know more clearly how vital you are to My purpose. There is work to be done, and I need you as a vessel through which to work. Not a vassal, but a vessel. I want to do a beautiful work.

Lo, I wait for you. Come to Me.

from *Come Away My Beloved*

Soul's Rest

*[God] hath raised us up together, and made us sit together
in heavenly places in Christ Jesus.*
EPHESIANS 2:6

*W*hen the heart is at one with the Father, there comes an illumination of Spirit that transcends thought.

Learn to worship and you will have rest of soul; you will rise to a new place of fellowship, where you will be: made to "sit together in the heavenly places in Christ Jesus."

You will be taught by the Spirit. Yes, He will open the mysteries of the Word to you. By the Spirit will the treasures of the Word be revealed.

from *Come Away My Beloved*

Rewards of Devotion

*He that loveth me shall be loved of my Father, and I will love him,
and will manifest myself to him.*
JOHN 14:21

*A*s your soul turns to worship, let it be with one supreme desire: to bring Me your love. This is not a selfish demand on My part. I can ask of you a full portion, yes, unlimited devotion, because I am a giver, not a taker, and you will always find yourself enriched beyond your expectations whenever you give yourself to me in even a very limited way.

I ask you to give only to bless you more.

from *On the Highroad of Surrender*

KINDNESS

*Hope maketh not ashamed; because the love of God
is shed abroad in our hearts.*
ROMANS 5:5

*K*indness is like a rose, which though easily crushed and fragile, yet speaks a language of silent power. It is the same power that lies in the eyes of one who loves. It is the power that moves the hands of those who give alms.

Beauty comes to the inner soul as tenderness becomes the outer expression. Those who find it have captured the atmosphere of heaven and have brought to their human relationships the essence of God's holy love.

from *On the Highroad of Surrender*

THE SPIRITUAL REALM

Come unto me, all ye that labour and are heavy laden.
MATTHEW 11:28

*D*o not be concerned about failing people. Your only true concern should be that you not fail Me. I am making last-minute preparations for My soon-coming. Do not frustrate My plans for you by pursuing your own.

I want you walking and expressing in the spiritual realm. Cast aside your carnal reasoning. Cast aside even your consideration for people and the threat of disappointing them. Would you rather that I be disappointed, in preference to others? Can you not trust Me? Would I fail anyone?

from *On the Highroad of Surrender*

FAITH AND ACTION

According to your faith be it unto you.
MATTHEW 9:29

*M*y promises are of no avail to you except as you apply and appropriate them by faith. In your daily walk, you shall be victorious only to the degree that you trust Me. I can help you only as you ask.

I need those who have proved My sufficiency in personal experience to lead the suffering to the fountains of life.

Never begrudge time given to chronic complainers, but recognize in each encounter the opportunity to speak a word that may lead to their liberation. No case is too hard for Me.

from *Come Away My Beloved*

THESE ARE DAYS OF THE MOVING OF MY SPIRIT

I will send. . .not a famine of bread. . .but of hearing the words of the LORD.
AMOS 8:11

*B*e alert. Be on guard. Do not attempt to make a judgment as to who is hungry for more of God. At any moment an appetite long dormant may be aroused, and the longer it has been dormant, the more voracious it will be.

Give My Word—these are the days of the moving of My Spirit.

Stay clear—allow no obstruction. Growth will spring forth wherever the waters reach.

from *Come Away My Beloved*

BREAK LOOSE THE FETTERS

Ye shall receive power, after that the Holy Ghost is come upon you.
ACTS 1:8

August 18

*W*ith a strong and mighty hand I will bring My people out. As I brought the children of Israel out from the bondage of Pharaoh; with a yet greater form of liberation I will bring My people out from under the yoke of false prophets and the shackles of legalism. Do not be afraid to follow Me. For one of these days the Son of Man shall be revealed in power and great glory. Break loose the fetters. Walk forth in the conquering strength of My Holy Spirit.

from *Come Away My Beloved*

August 19

AN INSTRUMENT OF PRAISE

*In returning and rest shall ye be saved; in quietness and in
confidence shall be your strength.*
ISAIAH 30:15

O My child, I have chosen you for Myself, that I may make you an instrument of praise in My hand. I will bring forth from you a melody of praise and rejoicing, and cause the harp strings of your soul to vibrate with a joyful song.

Bless Me with your lips, and whisper My Name in adoration. I will free you from the prison house, and you will exalt your God in liberty of spirit.

from *Come Away My Beloved*

LIVING IN JOY

Let them be confounded and consumed that are adversaries to my soul. . . .
And [I] will yet praise thee more and more.
PSALM 71:13–14

*W*hen you are baptized into His Spirit, evil loses its power to destroy you, darkness is dispelled, and the broken spirit healed. Joy is a balm that soothes the soul and lifts the burden from the grieving heart. Joy will be your saving grace, and praise your meat and drink. Only a joyful heart can worship Me in a way pleasing in My sight.

To weep and mourn is needless waste.

from On the Highroad of Surrender

A LIVING SACRIFICE

David would not drink of [the water], but poured it out to the LORD.
I CHRONICLES 11:18

*Y*ou are aware when My Spirit rejoices within you. This is My joy. This is the joy I promised. This is the greatest joy that can come to the human heart, for it is the joy of God.

Surely you will not only rejoice but be exceeding glad, with a gladness surpassing your power to tell.

In this way you will give this back to Me, even as David poured out to Me the precious water from the well of Bethlehem.

from Come Away My Beloved

RELEASE THE BLESSINGS ALSO

That good thing which was committed unto thee keep by the Holy Ghost.
2 TIMOTHY 1:14

August 22

*G*ive Me daily all that blesses. I will bless it and protect it.

All rest of heart comes through committal. You have been taught to release your burdens. Part of your anxiety at this moment has come from a feeling of responsibility to the care of that priceless thing which I Myself have given you. So I say: Give it to Me! I will not take it from you, but I will keep it for you, and thus it shall be twice blessed.

from *Progress of Another Pilgrim*

August 23

THE MYSTERY OF RIGHTEOUSNESS

For we wrestle not against flesh and blood, but against principalities,
against powers, against the rulers of the darkness of this world,
against spiritual wickedness in high places.
EPHESIANS 6:12

*G*race is the fullness of My love poured out upon the loveless. Return unto Me, and I will forgive your iniquities and heal your backslidings.

There is no peace in the heart of the transgressor and no joy in his spirit. But though you leave Me, I have not left you. You have chosen death, but I have chosen for you life in its abundance.

Do not faint, My child, and do not forsake the way of the Spirit for the way of the flesh.

from *On the Highroad of Surrender*

THE MOTIVATION OF LOVE

Though I speak with the tongues of men and of angels, and have not charity,
I am become as sounding brass, or a tinkling cymbal.
I CORINTHIANS 13:1

*M*any a life could be simplified and enriched by doing less and loving more. Indeed, all that is ever done, if not motivated by divine love, is in vain. It is worse than doing nothing, for it is potentially destructive.

There are those who have risen to fame through their noble acts, only to fall into shame and disrepute because of a bitter spirit.

from *Progress of Another Pilgrim*

_____

_____

_____

_____

_____

THE DIVINE COMMISSION

August 25

Go ye into all the world, and preach the gospel.
MARK 16:15

*M*y child, do not chafe at the bit. It is I who have put it in your mouth. You question My direction. But I would have you take a path that is quite different from the paths of your friends, and it is because I would bring you into a place in Me and a ministry in which they have no part.

Do not hesitate, and do not falter. Be gripped with one consuming purpose—to find the place I have for you.

from *Come Away My Beloved*

_____

_____

_____

_____

_____

August 26

RIGHTEOUSNESS, PEACE, AND JOY

*The kingdom of God is. . .righteousness, and peace, and joy in the
Holy Ghost. For he that in these things serveth Christ is acceptable
to God, and approved of men.*
ROMANS 14:17–18

*B*elieve Me and trust Me. You need not plot and scheme and plan. To doubt and to strive is to detain the Spirit. He needs not your help—only your submission. Give it willingly and gladly; yes, give it quickly, for the kingdom of God is righteousness, peace, and joy in the Holy Ghost, and you hinder the Spirit when these are not ruling your heart.

from *On the Highroad of Surrender*

August 27

FOREWARNED AND FOREARMED

I press toward the mark for the prize.
PHILIPPIANS 3:14

*N*ever waver once you have clear guidance. If you set out to do what I have bidden and sudden fear grips your heart, know that it is a device of the enemy. I am not the author of fear but of courage and a settled mind.

Confusion is the dust raised by the feet of the devil, calculated to cloud your vision and blind your eyes to the good I have placed directly in your path, and which you will surely find if you continue to act in faith.

from *On the Highroad of Surrender*

AN OPEN VESSEL

Now the God of hope fill you with all joy and peace in believing,
that ye may abound in hope, through the power of the Holy Ghost.
ROMANS 15:13

$\mathcal{B}$e about My business. Hold back nothing from Me. The fullness of My blessing moves through the sensitivity of your soul. The callous block Me out. It is not that I do not care for them, but it is that I find no response.

Give Me an open vessel into which I may pour My Spirit. Though it be of clay, it shall overflow with glory.

from *On the Highroad of Surrender*

THE APPLE OF MY EYE

He that heareth my word, and believeth on him that sent me,
hath everlasting life, and shall not come into condemnation;
but is passed from death unto life.
JOHN 5:24

$\mathcal{Y}$ou are the apple of My eye; I will guard you from harm. Never let the fears that are common to the world creep into your hearts, for you are not of the world.

You need not fear the coming judgment, for if your sins have been confessed and forgiven and cleansed by the blood of Jesus, you will not be condemned, because you are already passed from death into eternal life.

from *Come Away My Beloved*

FAITH, A PERPENDICULAR OPERATION

He that doubteth is damned if he eat, because he eateth not of faith:
for whatsoever is not of faith is sin.
ROMANS 14:23

August 30

*G*ive Me your trouble, whatever it may be. There is no disturbance big enough to warrant your distress, because anything committed to Me will be taken care of.

Truly live and walk by faith. I will be with you and I will be your strength.

No barrier shall stand in your way, because faith is a perpendicular operation. Your faith reaches straight up to Me, and My power comes straight down upon the place of action.

from *Progress of Another Pilgrim*

_____

_____

_____

_____

_____

August 31

SPIRITUAL RICHES

But covet earnestly the best gifts.
1 CORINTHIANS 12:31

*Y*ou can never ask beyond My power to provide.

Ask then, with complete confidence, but in all you desire, let it be for the enrichment of your soul. Seek not the treasures of the world, for they are transient.

Learn the value of spiritual riches, and set your heart to their attainment. As I bestow upon you spiritual enablements, I will use in a new way and in accordance with My highest purposes whatever lies within you of native abilities, or I may give you something entirely new. Nothing is wasted.

from *On the Highroad of Surrender*

_____

_____

_____

_____

_____

SOUND THE TRUMPET

Blow ye the trumpet in Zion, and sound an alarm in my holy mountain. . .
for the day of the LORD cometh, for it is nigh at hand.
JOEL 2:1

September 1

*B*e alert. Be vigilant. Sound the alarm from My holy mountain. Challenge my people that they be not overtaken by the enemy because they have a false sense of security. By My Spirit you shall overcome, and by My Word you shall prevail.

Gird on the armor of My holiness, and speak the word of faith. Victory is yours. I will send My delivering angel to stand beside you.

from *On the Highroad of Surrender*

SUFFERINGS AHEAD

September 2

Who now rejoice in my sufferings for you, and fill up that which is behind of the
afflictions of Christ in my flesh for his body's sake, which is the church.
COLOSSIANS 1:24

*T*here are sufferings yet to be accomplished in the body of the Church that I was not able to suffer on the cross. Be patient, hold steady through the days that lie ahead, and know that the trials and suffering are working toward a consuming glory.

Praise Me when the most difficult thing to do is to praise. This is the victory that overcomes the world.

from *Come Away My Beloved*

September 3

THE VINEYARD OF PRAYER

He maketh intercession for the saints according to the will of God.
ROMANS 8:27

The days are heavy with burdens that need to be borne upon the shoulders of faithful prayer warriors. Where are those who are willing to make themselves available for this ministry? You cannot in yourself lay this ministry upon your soul, but as you place yourself at the disposal of the Holy Spirit, He will use you as a channel when the needs arise.

I am calling My Spirit-filled believers to labor in the vineyard of prayer. Rejoice to be granted so sacred a task.

from *Come Away My Beloved*

September 4

RELY ON MY FAITHFULNESS

[You] are kept by the power of God through faith.
I PETER 1:5

Do not be anxious. My Spirit shall direct your steps. You need have no fear. There is never a place where you walk that I have not preceded you. There are many times when your faith wavers. Take no account of it. I am keeping you even when you do not feel strong. You must rely on My faithfulness—not on your feelings.

Your strength will vary from day to day, but My power is always available to you as you yield to the Holy Spirit.

from *Progress of Another Pilgrim*

FLESH AND BLOOD

Flesh and blood cannot inherit the kingdom of God.
I CORINTHIANS 15:50

*W*hatsoever is of the flesh is flesh;
but when you allow My Spirit to have free course,
then those things that shall be accomplished
both within and through you
will be truly the life of God.
For My Spirit is the Spirit of Life.

from *Come Away My Beloved*

_____

_____

_____

_____

_____

THE DYNAMIC OF MIRACLES

September 6

But ye shall receive power, after that the Holy Ghost is come upon you.
ACTS 1:8

*O*My child, lie quietly in My hand. The dynamic of miracles is here. Your own weakness is of no consequence, for I would vest you with My power. Your insignificance shall be swallowed up in My Presence.

My Presence is all about you, even all through you. Unless you resist Me, you cannot fail, for I cannot fail and you are in Me, kept by the power of God. Strengthen your heart with this truth.

from *Progress of Another Pilgrim*

_____

_____

_____

_____

_____

September 7

A FRESH MOVE OF FAITH

No man, having put his hand to the plough, and looking back,
is fit for the kingdom of God.
LUKE 9:62

*B*elieve Me for new things. Venture forth in trust. It is time to thrust forward in a new spearhead, a fresh move of faith. Fight procrastination as you would resist evil, for surely it is the enemy of good.

Put forth your hand to the plow and look not back, neither count the cost. I will repay you in the currency of eternity. Keep your eyes on Me and walk humbly.

from *On the Highroad of Surrender*

September 8

A DOOR OF UTTERANCE

They went forth, and preached every where, the Lord working with them,
and confirming the word with signs following.
MARK 16:20

*B*ehold, I set before you a door of utterance. You shall open your mouth, and I will fill it. You shall glorify Me, and your own vessel shall be an open channel for the river of My grace.

You shall bring healing [and] hope. I shall endue you with power from on high, and I shall magnify My word so that as you speak it forth I will confirm it, even with miracles following.

from *Progress of Another Pilgrim*

LAUNCH OUT

*And when Peter was come down out of the ship,
he walked on the water, to go to Jesus.*
MATTHEW 14:29

*L*aunch out, yea, launch out upon
My mighty power and limitless resources,
For, lo, if you would enter into all that I have for you,
    you must walk by faith upon the waters.
    You must relinquish forever your doubts.
For I will carry you, and I will sustain you by My power.

from *Come Away My Beloved*

FRUGALITY AND SUPPLY

September 10

*Better is little with the fear of the LORD than great treasure
and trouble therewith.*
PROVERBS 15:16

*Y*ou shall have My blessing as you bear the yoke, and in carrying My burdens there shall always be joy. I have called you for this ministry, and I will supply your needs so that you will not be weighed down with financial cares. Be willing to do without until I supply. Such as is needful I will give.

Learn to discern the difference between necessities and luxuries, and be content with modest things.

from *Progress of Another Pilgrim*

THE FORCES OF INTERCESSION

We know not what we should pray for as we ought: but the Spirit itself maketh intercession for us with groanings which cannot be uttered.
ROMANS 8:26

September 11

*B*ring the struggles within your soul to Me in prayer. It is the movement within you of the forces of intercession which you are feeling. It is not a personal struggle. The resolutions shall come as you pray, not as you search for wisdom as an end in itself.

Seek Me, and you shall know. You shall understand more than you dream possible, and your inner peace shall deepen.

from *Progress of Another Pilgrim*

September 12

RESIGNATION

Seek ye first the kingdom of God.
MATTHEW 6:33

*I*ncline your heart to Me, and attune your ear to My voice. For I have an urgent message to give you.

Do not set out to establish your own designs. I have already set in motion My divine will and purpose, and I would not have you interfere.

Resign all into My hands—your loved ones as well as your own self. Be obedient to the still small voice. Fret not about carnal things, but concern yourself first and always with spiritual values.

from *Come Away My Beloved*

SINCERITY

He is a rewarder of them that diligently seek him.
HEBREWS 11:6

*O*f the flesh, nothing spiritual can ever be produced.

This is why I said I loathed your sacrifices. It was not that I despised the ordinance in itself, but I perceived that it was an expression of self-righteousness, showing your indifference to the claim of God upon your heart.

My ordinances are to be entered into with deep sincerity and with awareness of their true significance. To sacrifice in carelessness and ignorance is to damage your own soul. Let your spirit never become callous.

from *Come Away My Beloved*

A WAY-PREPARER

September 14

Watch ye, stand fast in the faith, quit you like men, be strong.
1 CORINTHIANS 16:13

*B*e tolerant of all, at whatever stage of spiritual development they may be, but do not set your standards by theirs. I am moving, and I want you to be a way-preparer. Get into the front ranks, and hold your position. Never flinch. Certainly I can expect you never to turn coward and flee!

Give Me the privilege of sustaining you in the dangerous position. Think you not that I am well able to keep you there and adequately supply every needed grace?

from *Progress of Another Pilgrim*

CHALLENGE AND GROWTH

This kind goeth not out but by prayer and fasting.
MATTHEW 17:21

September 15

*I*n all the challenges of life, My hand is outstretched to give you courage. No stress need overwhelm if your confidence is in Me. To lean upon the arm of flesh brings certain disaster.

When the Psalmist penned, "From the Lord comes my help," he excluded all other sources. Effective faith is born of total consecration. My Spirit alone can bring forth this kind of dedication and inner strength.

Continual challenges bring constant growth.

Hold before Me at all times a heart that prefers instruction to comfort.

from *On the Highroad of Surrender*

September 16

RECOGNITION AND FOCUS

Beholding as in a glass the glory of the Lord,
[we] are changed into the same image.
2 CORINTHIANS 3:18

*R*ecognition, My child, brings Me into focus. Your motives concern Me; for I know that from pure motives spring good works.

Recognition is the sight I give your inner eye to discern distortion of My image in your own character. I would have your personality patterns display My character, and wherever this fails to be so, there is distortion of the image, and as others look to you for guidance and inspiration, they do not see a clear image of Me.

from *On the Highroad of Surrender*

THE FRUITS OF THE SPIRIT

The fruit of the Spirit is love, joy, peace, longsuffering, gentleness,
goodness, faith, meekness, temperance.
GALATIANS 5:22–23

*M*y presence within you, My divine life, operating in your human heart, creates the fruits of the Spirit.

It is not by self-effort that these heavenly attributes are brought forth. Verily the fruits of the Spirit are not native to the world.

Love, joy, and peace: these were natural to Jesus, but they are foreign to man's fallen nature. I am able to bring them forth even from your inmost being as you allow Me to live in you.

from *Progress of Another Pilgrim*

THE FATHER'S HUSBANDRY

September 18

I am the true vine, and my Father is the husbandman.
JOHN 15:1

*F*aith, meekness, temperance are fruits that mature slowly, and they are perfected by the careful husbandry of the Father. The faith which is produced within you as fruit of the Holy Spirit is a faith operating in the life of the believer to the end that he becomes a productive vehicle for the doing of the Father's work. And this fruit of meekness goes beyond mildness of temperament, even to an acceptance of injustice. It is not only patient, but gracious.

from *Progress of Another Pilgrim*

GOD'S PURPOSE

Why callest thou me good? there is none good but one, that is, God.
MATTHEW 19:17

*G*od's purpose in making you holy involves His own glory. He is not waiting to hear you called holy; He is listening to hear you call Him holy. He is not interested in making you a reputation, but in making you a disciple.

The rich young ruler flattered Jesus by addressing him as "good master," and Jesus rebuked him, pressing upon him the necessity to decide either to not call him good, or to acknowledge His deity. How then can He be pleased that one should desire such a reputation?

from On the Highroad of Surrender

September 20

SALVATION

Work out your own salvation with fear and trembling.
For it is God which worketh in you both to will and to do of his good pleasure.
PHILIPPIANS 2:12–13

*W*hen you are conscious of spiritual weakness, do not wait for Me to move upon you to effect a change from without, but assume the responsibility for your weakened condition as though you were indeed your own saviour. In the self-same moment, My grace will do the rest!

Wholeness is the product of the Spirit, but it cannot come until your own desire sets it in motion.

from Progress of Another Pilgrim

The Larger Life

I rather glory in my infirmities, that the power of Christ may rest upon me.
2 Corinthians 12:9

Never let your inadequacies be a handicap. Give them to Me, and they will become My opportunity to demonstrate My power operating through you. I would never have a chance to help you if you were always self-sufficient and capable of meeting every challenge.

Be ready to move in faith every time you sense inadequacy, and in each experience, as you trust Me, you will experience what is meant by "the larger life." I will fill all your lack with My divine undertaking.

from *Progress of Another Pilgrim*

The Door Is Open

September 22

*A great door and effectual is opened unto me,
and there are many adversaries.*
1 Corinthians 16:9

My child, the door is open. You shall go through by My grace and in My strength. Never gauge the possibilities of victory by examining your own strength. I am your Life, your Purity, your Wisdom, and your Strength. You have built faith for many years through a knowledge of and confidence in My Word. Now, I say unto you, put it into operation by walking in the path of action.

Move out, and trust Me as you go.

from *On the Highroad of Surrender*

September 23

BLESSING IN ADVERSITY

Sufferings of this present time are not worthy to be compared
with the glory which shall be revealed.
ROMANS 8:18

*A*dversities are a necessity. They are part of the pattern of life's pilgrimage for every individual; and who can escape them? But I say to you, that for those who walk in Me, and for those who are encircled by the intercessory prayers of My children, I will make of the suffering, yes, I will make of the trials a steppingstone to future blessing (see 2 Corinthians 4:17, 18).

My arms are around you, and never have I loved you more!

from *Come Away My Beloved*

September 24

PURITY OF MOTIVE

Though I have all faith. . .and have not charity, I am nothing.
1 CORINTHIANS 13:2

*R*egardless of how sacred may be the nature of a ministry, it may be marred by a heart that is selfish or impure. Whatever does not spring out of pure love becomes only a hollow noise.

Let those who desire to serve continually offer up a yielded vessel that I may fill it with love. Only thus is it possible for any man to enter into the activity of the Spirit of God in a way that furthers the divine purpose.

from *Progress of Another Pilgrim*

THE SPIRITUAL HOUSE

We are labourers together with God: ye are God's husbandry,
ye are God's building.
1 CORINTHIANS 3:9

*E*ach life is like the building of a house. Much labor is required in preparing the foundation. I build slowly and carefully, and you need patience, for years may pass before the superstructure of your spiritual house begins to take shape.

The swiftness with which I build is determined by your reception of truth. Truth assimilated generates creativity. Obedience practiced generates productivity. Therefore, a teachable spirit and determined desire to do My will hastens the working of My purposes in you.

from On the Highroad of Surrender

PRAISE AND REPROOF

September 26

Behold, thou art fair, my love; behold, thou art fair.
SONG OF SOLOMON 1:15

*M*y child, do not let the words of others influence you unduly—neither their praise nor their criticism. Weigh each for its proper value, and come back to Me. Only in communion with Me can you be sure of the truth. If I correct you, it is for your betterment. If I encourage you it is because I know you need it.

The more you find of the truth about your own self, the more you will be set free from improper evaluations of your worth, free from false pride that seeks to cover recognized flaws.

I want your life, character, and personality to be as beautiful and lovely as I visualized you to be when I created you.

from Come Away My Beloved

PATIENCE AND PERFECTION

Let patience have her perfect work.
JAMES 1:4

*P*atience is not a matter of forethought nor self-control. It will manifest itself quite naturally and without effort when the soul is rid of all resentment against imperfection. Purity of heart is possible but perfection is a word that could have been used to describe only a few rare souls, and then only relatively.

The only way you can make any reasonable progress toward perfection is by committing your entire life into My hands and realizing it is I who live within you and effect whatever changes are made.

from *Progress of Another Pilgrim*

September 28

INNER STRENGTH AND OUTER ACTION

He that covereth his sins shall not prosper:
but whoso confesseth and forsaketh them shall have mercy.
PROVERBS 28:13

*I*ntegrity and devotion have always been indispensable virtues. I say to you that in this hour of apathy and decline when the very foundations of mankind's moral structures are crumbling, you need to be more diligent than ever to find and to keep your own personal inner strength and to allow it to manifest in outer action.

from *Progress of Another Pilgrim*

Do Not Gather Fire

Can a man take fire in his bosom, and his clothes not be burned?
PROVERBS 6:27

*H*ave I not said you should pray much that you might not enter into temptation?

I desire always to help, but many pray too late; for by their own careless actions they have placed their feet in a slippery path, and the results are almost inevitable.

Do not gather fire into your garments and pray not to be burned, nor take up a serpent and ask for protection. Give the devil wide berth, and spare the soul much unnecessary anguish.

from *On the Highroad of Surrender*

Dependence on God

September 30

*We are made partakers of Christ, if we hold. . .
our confidence stedfast unto the end.*
HEBREWS 3:14

*D*o not walk carelessly, nor lay out your own paths on which to travel. You cannot know what lies in the distance. So walk closely with Me, that you may be able to draw quickly upon My aid. No matter how well-developed your faith is, never think for a moment that you need My support any less.

Move forward with courage and confidence; but always allow Me to walk ahead, and choose the right path.

from *Come Away My Beloved*

October 1

GUARD AGAINST FOOLISHNESS

By thy words thou shalt be justified,
and by thy words thou shalt be condemned.
MATTHEW 12:37

*G*uard your own spirit against foolishness. Thoughts of nonsense and empty words are utter waste.

All words are either actively good or actively negative, and if they are negative, they are destructive. They will nullify the testimony I would establish when you speak My words, so that if you mix the two, the good will be cancelled out by the evil.

You cannot afford such carelessness. Let your every word be full of grace and taste of the saltiness of divine goodness.

from *Progress of Another Pilgrim*

October 2

AVOID FRIVOLITY

Every idle word that men shall speak, they shall give account thereof.
MATTHEW 12:36

*A*void frivolity with the same carefulness as you disdain the grosser sins. The latter are transgressions of the law of God, but the former is a thief and will rob both yourself and others of spiritual good.

A bantering spirit may cause you to be oblivious to opportunities to minister that may lie directly in your path. Thus if you are indulging in spiritual profligacy, you rob the other person of the blessing you could have given, and you rob yourself of the reward you would have received.

from *Progress of Another Pilgrim*

LOVE AND VAIN RELIGION

Love thy neighbour as thyself.
JAMES 2:8

*H*e who does not express love exposes the darkness of his soul, though he be clothed with religion. "This man's religion is vain," wrote James, if he does not express his faith by kindness and good deeds (James 1:26–27). He needs no man to condemn him; he condemns himself by his failure to show consideration for the feelings of his brother. He has appointed himself to a high place and is scarcely fit for the lowest.

"But he that is greatest among you shall be your servant," said Jesus (Matthew 23:11).

from *Make Haste My Beloved*

SHARE COURAGE

October 4

To the weak became I as weak, that I might gain the weak.
1 CORINTHIANS 9:22

*S*elf-dependence makes it difficult to comprehend the timidity of the weak. Though you may have gained a measure of strength, remember that it was not native; it has been cultivated through a multitude of experiences, and you can remember many times when you were fearful and trembling. Other souls are still in the place of fear and desperation. Be always ready and willing to stand with them in that place and share your faith and courage!

from *On the Highroad of Surrender*

365
ONE-MINUTE MEDITATIONS

October 5

STRENGTH AND WEAKNESS

Of him are ye in Christ Jesus, who of God is made unto us wisdom,
and righteousness, and sanctification, and redemption: that. . .
He that glorieth, let him glory in the Lord.
1 CORINTHIANS 1:30–31

*M*y Spirit within you is the source of your spiritual life and strength. Look not to your own natural abilities, for My Spirit empowers the one who would walk in faith, so that he who is weak need not despair, and he who feels himself to be strong shall learn not to boast; for I bring down the mighty and make strong the weak.

from *On the Highroad of Surrender*

October 6

RECOGNIZE THE ENEMY

Be ye not unequally yoked together with unbelievers.
2 CORINTHIANS 6:14

*H*ear My voice. My Word is all you need. Study more and be filled with its wisdom that you may be fortified against insidious attacks of fallacious human reasoning. The high-sounding phrases of the humanist seem convincing at times. But I say to you that any search that leads you to your own self rather than to Me is of the devil. Either take the offensive and win a victory for Me, or else sever the connection. It would be better to retreat than to fall into a snare.

from *On the Highroad of Surrender*

MAGNIFICENT GIFT

Walk in the Spirit, and ye shall not fulfil the lust of the flesh.
GALATIANS 5:16

*W*ell I know the instability of the human heart and natural affection. Thus I have supplied My own love to thy heart by the indwelling of My Holy Spirit. He it is who testifies of Me. He it is who prompts thy worship, who kindles the fires of devotion, who constantly draweth thee to Myself.

Do ye long to love Me more deeply? Seek the infilling of My Holy Spirit. In this one magnificent gift, I have made full provision for thine every need.

from *Dialogues with God*

_____

_____

_____

_____

_____

A HOLY TEMPLE

October 8

Who shall ascend into the hill of the LORD? or who shall stand in his holy place?
He that hath clean hands, and a pure heart.
PSALM 24:3–4

*Y*our heart is the citadel of the Holy Spirit. I hold the keys to every chamber and will keep out every evil thing if you do not invite the enemy. I desire for you a holy temple.

Give Me your adoration from a pure heart and let no ulterior motives invade your personal sanctuary, for I desire truth in the depths of the soul and the divided heart cannot worship.

from *On the Highroad of Surrender*

_____

_____

_____

_____

OUTFLOW

What is a man profited, if he shall gain the whole world,
and lose his own soul?
MATTHEW 16:26

*T*he spirit is prepared for worldly success only after it has learned to care nothing for it. I fill the hand that lies open in worship. The hand that grasps shall be forever empty. Learn to leave to My love and wisdom all your destiny. Nothing ought concern you but the health of your soul and the outflow of your life. You will free your soul as you refuse to seek anything and desire only to give. Then shall I bless you.

from *On the Highroad of Surrender*

October 10

CRISIS EXPERIENCES

But the God of all grace, who hath called us unto his eternal glory by Christ Jesus,
after that ye have suffered a while, make you perfect, stablish, strengthen, settle you.
I PETER 5:10

I will never leave you alone in the midst of any affliction. You cannot escape the crisis experiences if you desire to grow and mature, but you need never fear them regardless of the form they take, for My grace and My equanimity shall be as a strong anchor that shall hold you fast, and you shall not be driven off course.

from *Progress of Another Pilgrim*

A RAIN OF FIRE

The time is come that judgment must begin.
I PETER 4:17

A rain of fire is falling, a rain of judgment upon My house. It is My people whom I am purifying now.

I shall send the fire as you wait upon Me. It shall bring you refreshing as a rain. It shall be death to the old carnal nature, but it shall be life to the inner man—the new nature that is yours in Christ.

Never be afraid of My judgments. I do not send them in wrath upon My church, but in love and compassion.

from *Make Haste My Beloved*

THE ECHO OF MY VOICE

Ye make clean the outside of the cup and of the platter,
but within they are full of extortion and excess.
MATTHEW 23:25

*T*he cry of your soul is the echo of My voice calling you to repentance. Your love for Me will place you under My chastening rod, for as long as you love Me, you will seek My face even when you anticipate My reproach.

Let Me deal with any unsoundness in your spirit, and I will spare you the humiliation of open shame. Inner conviction comes through My Word, and this is your only sure way of finding peace in My presence.

from *On the Highroad of Surrender*

October 13

No Fear

Fear not, little flock; for it is your Father's good pleasure
to give you the kingdom.
LUKE 12:32

*N*o, My children, do not fear. I am not simply preserving you, but I am doing so for the purpose of sharing with you My kingdom power. If you can catch the vision of what the days ahead hold in store for you in My great kingdom, you will gain a whole new perspective, so that as you view the present, transient scene, its true dimension will come into focus in proportion to the whole panoramic picture.

from *Come Away My Beloved*

October 14

Closed Doors

I give unto you power. . .over all the power of the enemy: and nothing shall. . .hurt you.
LUKE 10:19

*N*ever lose heart when confronted by disappointment.

Remember always that I control all that touches you, and as I move to order your life, I not only open the right doors, but close the wrong ones. Whenever a wrong door is closed, it is by My hand as much as when a right one opens. In this way I not only bring you joy but spare you pain. Trust Me.

Have I not said that nothing shall harm you?

from *On the Highroad of Surrender*

I Await Your Desire

Sell all that thou hast, and distribute unto the poor,
and thou shalt have treasure in heaven: and come, follow me.
LUKE 18:22

I rejoice in ministering to an open heart. I have so much to give and so few truly desire to receive. I would give so much more abundantly if they would but ask.

I await your desire, because if I gave to you when your desire was small, you would not be prepared for receiving.

Bring Me everything, and repent of anything you cannot offer Me as a holy gift. Release all to Me.

from *Progress of Another Pilgrim*

Physical Health and Spiritual Ministry

October 16

I wish. . .that thou mayest prosper and be in health, even as thy soul prospereth.
3 JOHN 1:2

D o not misconstrue the scripture which says "I beat my body to keep it in subjection." A more clear way to state the true intent would be to say, "By proper discipline and care of the physical body, it may be made to fulfill the desires and demands of the soul." Otherwise, you may by lack of concern for your physical health, hamper your spiritual ministry.

Run the race with a pure heart, and the reward shall be given you.

from *Progress of Another Pilgrim*

October 17

ONE DAY AT A TIME

Take therefore no thought for the morrow:
for the morrow shall take thought for the things of itself.
MATTHEW 6:34

*O*My child, have you not known the way of the Lord, and can you not trust Him now? Nothing shall befall you but that which comes from His hand. No one shall set upon you to hurt you, for your God has built around you a wall of fire.

Be content with what each day brings, rejoicing in your God, for surely He shall deliver you. He is the One who has brought you here.

His heart is surely your strong tower.

from *Come Away My Beloved*

October 18

SIMPLICITY OF SPIRIT

Whosoever shall not receive the kingdom of God as a little child
shall in no wise enter therein.
LUKE 18:17

*B*y simplicity of spirit the soul is protected against forces of destruction. He who clings to My hand in childlike trust shall walk with joy in a path of safety. He who seeks to preserve his own soul by the devices of his own intellect will be snared and brought into confusion and bondage.

Give yourself to love Me and to worship Me. The results in your soul will be joy and victory.

from *Progress of Another Pilgrim*

The Law of Plenty

As poor, yet making many rich; as having nothing,
and yet possessing all things.
2 CORINTHIANS 6:10

*I*t matters not how little you have of the treasures of the world, for if you are blessed with the bounty of My grace, you shall be always a giver. There is no want for him who is My follower. There is no lack for him who has found that he can buy wine and milk without money and without price (Isaiah 55:1). He has found the law of plenty who has found Me as his source. He shall find abundance crowding his pathway.

from *On the Highroad of Surrender*

Thorns in the Nest

Our light affliction. . .worketh for us a far more exceeding
and eternal weight of glory.
2 CORINTHIANS 4:17

I control the forces that bear upon your life. Do not question circumstances. Look to Me for an understanding of your inner responses.

While you are praying for a problem to be solved, a need to be met, a thorn to be removed from your nest, I am watching for true faith to express in the time of want, and I am waiting to see when the thorns in the nest will cause you to move out and try your unused wings.

from *Progress of Another Pilgrim*

FOLLY OF IMMATURITY

And that ye put on the new man,
which after God is created in righteousness and true holiness.
EPHESIANS 4:24

*I*t is so simple when you approach Me in proper fashion and do not hinder your spiritual progress by regression to a parent-child position in your attitude. I know full well when you are no longer properly in that stage, and although you may attempt to fall back into it to avoid responsibility, I will not respond, and you will be left to a folly of your own making.

from On the Highroad of Surrender

October 22

HOLINESS UPON THE HEART

He hath chosen us in him before the foundation of the world,
that we should be holy and without blame before him in love.
EPHESIANS 1:4

I the Lord have tried you. I have given you the freedom to choose either good or evil. Be not deceived. Though you see no eye, you are being looked upon, and though you seek no voice, I continue to call.

Turn to Me, My child. Open your heart to My grace. Holiness shall be written upon the hearts of My people. They shall minister in power because they live in obedience.

from On the Highroad of Surrender

THE ROAD IS STEEP

Strait is the gate, and narrow is the way, which leadeth unto life.
MATTHEW 7:14

*Y*ou are a chosen vessel to Me, so do not be filled with filthy lucre. Be wholesome, humble, simple; for simplicity and a spirit of humility befit one who serves the Lord.

You are My treasure. I delight in you when you are fully yielded to Me with no thoughts of personal ambition or achievement. If you wish for anything, wish for more of My nearness. If you long after anything, long after more of My righteousness and more of My love.

from *Come Away My Beloved*

_____

_____

_____

_____

_____

GRIEF

October 24

Sufferings of this present time are not worthy to be compared
with the glory which shall be revealed.
ROMANS 8:18

*T*here is a river of divine grace flowing beneath all your need. Under your deepest sorrow moves My compassion and My love. In a very real sense, you fathom the depth of My own heart only to the extent that your heart is broken and your inmost consciousness torn asunder by the pain of grief.

Never look upon trials and tests and disciplines as being damaging. Whatever hurt they seem to bring is outweighed by the blessing that follows.

from *On the Highroad of Surrender*

_____

_____

_____

_____

_____

October 25

BROKENNESS

Godly sorrow worketh repentance to salvation. . .
but the sorrow of the world worketh death.
2 CORINTHIANS 7:10

The storms of life may make shipwreck of a soul, but this may be purely destructive. The brokenness of spirit wrought by the hand of God becomes a constructive work. It is the godly sorrow unto repentance that brings Life.

True prayer is born out of brokenness. This brokenness is contrition for sins, tenderness of feeling, and gratitude for grace. If you let it work in your heart, it will surely draw you closer and closer to Me.

from On the Highroad of Surrender

October 26

KEEP YOUR CHANNEL CLEAR

The water that I shall give him shall be in him a well of water
springing up into everlasting life.
JOHN 4:14

Will I speak to you as one whose voice is lost in the noise of the crashing surf? Will you be like an instrument with broken strings from which the musician can bring forth no music?

No, I would have you be as the waterfall whose sound is continuous, as a great river whose flow is not interrupted.

from Come Away My Beloved

Pray and Walk in the Spirit

As many as are led by the Spirit of God, they are the sons of God.
Romans 8:14

October 27

I have admonished you to pray in the Spirit, but do not forget that I have also commanded you to WALK in the Spirit, and this I expect not part of the time, but all the time.

The need is critical, the hour is late, and I am calling for full commitment from My own. You have desired to be chosen. Having been chosen, I would have you understand that I expect far more of you than of those who are not.

from *Progress of Another Pilgrim*

Fulfillment

October 28

Herein is my Father glorified, that ye bear much fruit.
John 15:8

You have been like a green plant. Now I would have you put forth blossoms. The flowering is a symbol of the manifestation of the Spirit. Yes, it is even more; it is fulfillment of original purpose. It is the ultimate end to which it was designated by the Creator.

Only to have life is not enough. Fulfillment is that for which I am waiting, yes, the manifestation of My sons and daughters as they come to maturity and as they produce that for which I created them.

from *Progress of Another Pilgrim*

October 29

ANTICIPATE SURPRISES

The angel of the Lord spake unto Philip, saying, Arise, and go toward the south unto the way that goeth. . .unto Gaza, which is desert.
ACTS 8:26

*T*have purposes for you. I have a ministry for you. Look not to any man to open this door. I not only open doors, but more often than otherwise, I create the place of service. I lead in new paths and down unpaved roads.

One Bible example of this is the account of Philip and his witness to the eunuch crossing the desert.

Be prepared for the unexpected, and anticipate surprises.

from *Progress of Another Pilgrim*

October 30

STRIVINGS HINDER

If a man love me, he will keep my words: and my Father will love him, and we will come unto him.
JOHN 14:23

*M*y people are drifting like a boat with empty sails. But I shall blow, saith the Lord; yes, I shall cause a mighty wind to rise, and the sails shall be filled, and the Spirit shall drive you forward.

In your own power you can accomplish nothing whatsoever in the kingdom of God.

All strivings only hinder. Love is the only telling contribution you can make toward the perfecting of your soul.

from *Progress of Another Pilgrim*

Renew Your Vows

He that hath my commandments, and keepeth them,
he it is that loveth me.
JOHN 14:21

*T*here is a day coming when you will say, "I have waited in vain for the Lord." You will wait for Me to speak, and you will hear only the whistling of the wind. But I tell you now, I am never silent; you are deaf. I am always speaking; but I do not find your ear attuned to listen.

You have become insensitive to My presence.

Confess your coldness, and draw near to Me. Renew your vows, and I will revive your ministry.

from Come Away My Beloved

The Course Lies Dead Ahead

November 1

Thanks be to God, which giveth us the victory
through our Lord Jesus Christ.
I CORINTHIANS 15:57

*M*y Spirit broods upon the waters, even upon the waters of difficulty. Be not dismayed, neither be turned aside. Set your heart with even greater diligence to follow the Spirit. Others may find Me and lose Me again. Be not discouraged. What navigator would set his course by the location of other ships? You have a harbor to make, and you have a course to follow that lies dead ahead.

from Progress of Another Pilgrim

THE WAYS OF THE SPIRIT

The men which journeyed with him stood speechless,
hearing a voice, but seeing no man.
ACTS 9:7

*D*o not grieve My Spirit and do not quench His power when He is moving in your own or another vessel. My purifying work is being done in the sacred moments when My anointing is resting upon a soul. Be aware that as a witness, you stand on holy ground, and reverence should be your attitude.

Like Saul on the road to Damascus, to him were spoken clear words, while others heard only a sound.

from On the Highroad of Surrender

STAY BENEATH MY WING

When thou passest through the waters, I will be with thee.
ISAIAH 43:2

*W*ill I create, and will I not have it in My power to destroy? Is it not written that the potter breaks one vessel that He may shape a new one (see Jeremiah 18:4)? Yes, I will bring My will to pass, and man will know that his will is like a broken straw when pitted against the Almighty.

But My people will know the protection of their God. Stay beneath My wings, and I will make you a tower of strength.

from Come Away My Beloved

RUN WITH PATIENCE

Let us lay aside every weight, and. . .
run with patience the race that is set before us.
HEBREWS 12:1

I could by adversity strip from you the comforts of life, but I will bless you in double portion, if of your own accord you do as the apostle Paul and lay aside every weight, resisting the many temptations that continually beset you as you run with patience the course I set before you.

from *Come Away My Beloved*

_____

_____

_____

_____

_____

TAKE NO THOUGHT FOR TOMORROW

Consider the lilies of the field. . .they toil not, neither do they spin: and yet
. . .even Solomon in all his glory was not arrayed like one of these.
MATTHEW 6:28–29

*L*et go your earthly cares.
   I do not forbid you to work, only to worry. The best way to break the power of worry is to refuse to take thought for tomorrow. Today is rarely a problem. Most anxious thoughts are related to the future. Put all of tomorrow into My keeping.
   For today you need Wisdom. For tomorrow you need Faith.

from *Progress of Another Pilgrim*

_____

_____

_____

_____

_____

EXPECT THE UNEXPECTED

Philip went. . .and preached Christ unto them. And the people. . .
gave heed unto those things which Philip spake,
hearing and seeing the miracles which he did.
ACTS 8:5–6

*O*My child, let Me speak to you, and let My Spirit direct your life. I may lead you in unexpected ways, and ask things of you that are startling, but I will never guide you amiss.

You shall go as Philip went—at the direction of the Spirit—into the places that are out of the way, and bring light on My Word to those who are in need.

from *Come Away My Beloved*

SEERS

Take heed therefore how ye hear.
LUKE 8:18

*T*here is a spirit of bewilderment abroad in the land today that causes people to go about as though they were moving through a dense fog. Vision is obscured. Never have I needed watchmen, heralds, prophets, and seers as I need them in this hour.

Stay close to me no matter what attractions exert themselves to draw you away. Give fuller attention to the things of the Spirit.

You can never fail to hear My voice if your ears have been unstopped by obedience and the desire to please and serve Me.

from *On the Highroad of Surrender*

KEY TO JOY

*Whosoever will save his life shall lose it; but whosoever shall lose his life
for my sake and the gospel's, the same shall save it.*
MARK 8:35

Surrender is the key to joy. By release the soul is freed. Bondage is the twin of selfishness. To hold is to lose, and to free is to gain.

Meditation opens the door to revelation, and revelation brings liberation. Test it in any given situation. You will find that you hold in your own hand the instrument of life. It will work like a magic eye to open the heaviest door.

from *On the Highroad of Surrender*

ANGELS ARE SEPARATING

November 9

The harvest is the end of the world; and the reapers are the angels.
MATTHEW 13:39

You have been aware of the presence and ministry of angels. You, as believers, are being gathered unto the Father. Meanwhile the children of wrath and disobedience are being separated and gathered to each other.

Know this when you would wonder why one is brought in and another goes out never to return. Question it not, for you are seeing this prophecy fulfilled, at least in part. It shall be accelerated as the end draws nearer.

You shall find in this understanding much peace of heart.

from *Progress of Another Pilgrim*

November 10

ON DOING THE FATHER'S WORK

Every tree is known by his own fruit.
LUKE 6:44

There is a day coming when you will regret your lethargy, and you will ask, "Why did we leave the vineyard of the Lord untended?" Those things that have occupied you will appear for what they are—chaff and worthlessness.

I have fashioned you for better things. Do not fail Me. Place your life under My divine control and learn to live in the full blessing of My highest will.

I will strengthen you and comfort you; I will lead you by the hand.

from *Come Away My Beloved*

November 11

DISMISS WITH DISPATCH

Jesus. . .saith unto him, Go home to thy friends,
and tell them how great things the Lord hath done for thee.
MARK 5:19

Nothing I am doing would seem strange to you if you had been more attentive to My voice.

I can lead you only as you wait upon Me for guidance. Man will always take you down the wrong path. It is folly to stumble along in blindness. I am your friend. Can you not trust My love? Would I ever harm you? Do I not give you a full measure of joy?

from *Progress of Another Pilgrim*

Humbled Hearts

How canst thou say. . .Brother, let me pull out the mote that is in thine eye, when thou thyself beholdest not the beam that is in thine own eye?
LUKE 6:42

*Y*ou have listened to My words as though they were of little consequence. You cannot resist My Spirit without suffering pain; and you cannot turn a deaf ear to My words without falling into the snare of the enemy.

Look no more to My hand to supply freely your needs when you have not cleansed your hands and come to Me with a broken and a contrite heart.

from *Come Away My Beloved*

Affliction, No Stranger

November 13

Though he slay me, yet will I trust in him.
JOB 13:15

*A*ffliction is no stranger to the child of God. Darkness falls upon both saint and sinner. Those who know Me intimately will find a deep joy in the midst of life's bitterness.

I do not smooth out the way for My loved ones, for how then could they testify of My provision?

I prepare you in order to use you in the hour of crisis. The crisis is not the time to cry for deliverance, saying, "Lord, *save* me," but to cry, "Lord, *use* me."

from *On the Highroad of Surrender*

THE GIFT OF FORGIVENESS

Launch out into the deep, and let down your nets for a draught.
LUKE 5:4

*O*My child, come to Me—I want to give you a new gift. I want you to see all people as being under the shed sacrifice of the blood of Christ.

He has died for all. His forgiveness encompasses all. Tell them the Good News. It is the confidence in your own heart that will engender faith to receive within the hearts of others.

Freely forgive all, as you have freely loved all. Those to whom you extend My forgiveness will come to experience it for themselves.

from *Come Away My Beloved*

AN INJECTION OF NEW LIFE

Whom he did foreknow, he also did predestinate
to be conformed to the image of his Son.
ROMANS 8:29

*A*ll you do for Me in ministering to others is part of My own working within you; for whenever you bless another, you bring an injection of new life and vitality into your own spirit and personality.

Your character is that which I shape from the broken fragments of all your testings; therefore, accept the trials with a grateful heart. I will use all things to bring you into conformity to My image if you will trust Me.

from *Progress of Another Pilgrim*

HEART-PURITY

If we confess our sins, he is faithful and just to forgive.
I JOHN 1:9

*I*t is not by grieving over your sins that they are forgiven. My forgiveness is in constant operation and you need only accept it. The cleansing of your heart and the restoration of your joy depends upon your full confession and willingness to repent and to renounce your sin. Exercise your soul toward the achievement of heart-purity. Until this work is accomplished (and maintained), you will not have inner peace.

Seek My face in repentance until you have yielded to Me all that distresses you.

from *Come Away My Beloved*

GOD'S MERCY

Charity shall cover the multitude of sins.
I PETER 4:8

*I*f it is true that human love covers a multitude of sins, how much more true is it of the divine love of God the Father! Knowing My deep love for you, your own heart will no longer condemn you. My mercies are everlasting, My kindness, abundant.

My grace extends to the least of My children, and My tenderness shall make you strong. I go before you daily to prepare your way, and you will be accompanied by My goodness and My mercy.

from *Come Away My Beloved*

365

ONE-MINUTE MEDITATIONS

November 18

PERFECTING OF SOUL

Now the God of peace. . .make you perfect in every good work.
HEBREWS 13:20–21

*I*f you set up barriers through pride or self-defense, you hinder the progress of your soul. Be as a little child, and stay open to the flow of My life in you: so shall you be spared many a bitter disappointment and much weary striving. Only in this way can you keep your balance and poise. Thus shall your perfecting be accomplished.

Nothing you could ever do for Me can be more important than this—the perfecting of your own soul.

from *Progress of Another Pilgrim*

November 19

GODLY SORROW VERSUS CARNAL

A merry heart maketh a cheerful countenance:
but by sorrow of the heart the spirit is broken.
PROVERBS 15:13

*O*vermuch sorrow causes the heart to fail. If you would be a rejoicing Christian, the griefs of the carnal man must be laid aside.

To bemoan any unpleasant natural circumstance accomplishes nothing but a heaping up of misery. Undue distress about untoward happenings is devastating to the soul. The only kind of sorrow that I can use for your good is the godly sorrow of true repentance.

Turn to Me in every trial, and give it all to Me.

from *Progress of Another Pilgrim*

A Covert in the Storm

Humble yourselves. . .casting all your care upon him.
I Peter 5:6–7

*B*e at peace, for in Me there is a covert in the storm. My love remains changeless whatever winds may blow. My grace will sustain you however deep may be the night.

Nothing harms the trusting soul though calamity be his companion. In affliction there shall be comfort, for he who abides in Me shall not know desolation. I protect, I provide, I enrich. He who loves Me is supremely blessed; My grace is his strength, and I am his salvation.

from *On the Highroad of Surrender*

Tensions Build Fortitude

Blessed is the man that endureth temptation.
James 1:12

*M*any perplexities bring you closer to Me, for as you seek wisdom and need courage, you are driven to Me for help. These are the times you become pliable in My hands. It is the moments of crisis that reveal either a man's strength or his weakness. It is the tensions of life that build fortitude or expose fear.

Know that I keep you, that I love you, that I fully understand. Cast yourself wholly upon My mercy. Pray, knowing that the request is already granted and the help already provided.

from *Progress of Another Pilgrim*

ON THE WATERS OF SORROW

Eye hath not seen, nor ear heard, neither have entered into the heart of man,
the things which God hath prepared for them that love him.
1 CORINTHIANS 2:9

*J*am coming to you walking on the waters of the sorrows of your life; yes, above the sounds of the storm you shall hear My voice call your name.

Never despair, for I am watching over and caring for you. Be not anxious. I am working out the details of circumstances so that I may bless you and reveal Myself to you in a new way.

from *Come Away My Beloved*

THE SOUL IS DIRECTIONAL

Jesus. . .said unto her, Martha, Martha, thou art careful and troubled about many things: but one thing is needful:
and Mary hath chosen that good part, which shall not be taken away from her.
LUKE 10:41–42

*M*y people need direction. There are many pressures which influence them, but they need to hear a clear voice giving them the wisdom of God.

The soul is directional, and any heart turned toward Me in an attitude of true worship shall receive from Me a quickening flow of life. It cannot be otherwise.

from *Progress of Another Pilgrim*

THE HIGHROAD OF
ABSOLUTE SURRENDER

I am the way.
JOHN 14:6

*C*ome close to Me. I have consolations for your soul that surpass your sharpest grief. I have walked through the deepest waters, and I am with you as you experience your baptism of sorrow. It is the path that leads to the gate of glory, and the Father waits to greet you there. It is not heaven of which I speak. It is a blessedness of spirit given to those who have passed through tribulations and have set their feet on the highroad of absolute surrender. From this place there is no turning back.

from *On the Highroad of Surrender*

ENDURANCE

Hope maketh not ashamed; because the love of God is shed abroad
in our hearts by the Holy Ghost which is given unto us.
ROMANS 5:5

*M*y child, do not flinch under My disciplines. I never send more than you can endure. Can you accept the cup of suffering as readily as you embrace joy? You can do so in greater degrees as your trust in Me increases.

My love never fails, even when it brings you pain. It is in the patient endurance of affliction that the soul is seasoned with grace.

from *On the Highroad of Surrender*

THE BLESSINGS OF THE PURE IN HEART

Blessed are the pure in heart: for they shall see God.
MATTHEW 5:8

*I*s not My heart drawn out toward you to bless you? Yield your whole being to Me. I am your loving Father. I know your need even before it arises. My provisions are not only sure, but also full and overflowing, so that you may confess with the psalmist, "I shall never want." You will see with a vision denied to many, for your heart is pure, and to the pure of heart is given the promise that they shall see God.

from *Come Away My Beloved*

YOU CANNOT WEARY MY LOVE

Be not faithless, but believing.
JOHN 20:27

*L*ift your eyes, and look upon Me. For though you have forgotten Me, I have not forgotten you. While you have busied yourselves with your daily occupations, I have still been occupied with you.

You cannot weary My love. You may grieve My heart, but My love is changeless, infinite. I long for you to turn to Me. My hands are full of blessings that I desire to give you. I long to hear your voice. You speak much with others—O speak to Me! I have so much to tell you.

from *Come Away My Beloved*

ON PRIVACY

Charity suffereth long, and is kind. . .is not easily provoked, thinketh no evil.
1 CORINTHIANS 13:4–5

*D*o not allow your thoughts to pursue in curiosity what you do not understand in the lives of others.

To violate the spiritual privacy of another is a greater breach of ethics than to invade his house uninvited. Rest assured that if your friendship warrants, he will share with you as he deems wise.

Love believes only the best. There is no more eloquent way to express love and respect for another than by allowing him full liberty of independent action.

from On the Highroad of Surrender

HARMONY OF PURPOSE

November 29

Whosoever. . .forsaketh not all that he hath, he cannot be my disciple.
LUKE 14:33

*T*hose who seek to live in obedience to My commandments will be brought into conformity with My nature, and these will I use to fulfill My purposes. Do not men do likewise? When a man chooses a workman, he takes into account not only his natural capabilities for the task, but also whether or not there is harmony of thought, purpose, character, and vision. If a man's heart is not in his work, his abilities will not be enough in themselves to make him a success.

from Progress of Another Pilgrim

November 30

ONLY BY A PERSON

I am the living bread which came down from heaven: if any man
eat of this bread, he shall live for ever.
JOHN 6:51

I will bless you when your hearts turn to Me in earnestness and sincerity. From where shall your help come, except from the Lord? You search in vain for satisfaction from your worldly possessions.

Your soul can be nourished only by a person—not by any thing; and the only person adequate to meet the hunger of your soul is the Person of the Lord Jesus Christ, through the ministry of the blessed Holy Spirit.

from *Progress of Another Pilgrim*

December 1

CALL OF THE TURTLEDOVE

When Elisabeth heard the salutation of Mary, the babe leaped in her womb;
and Elisabeth was filled with the Holy Ghost.
LUKE 1:41

*T*here is the sound of the turtledove echoing throughout the land. It is the voice of the Bridegroom calling His Bride. It is the call of love, and those who truly love Him will respond.

In a world filled with noises, they will hear Him.

Like Elizabeth when she was greeted by Mary. The response was an inner, involuntary response to the nearness of the Christ.

Anticipate Me. Watch for Me. Your heart shall hear.

from *Come Away My Beloved*

Put Off the Self Life

If ye know these things, happy are ye if ye do them.
JOHN 13:17

*B*e aware of My presence. Your receptivity is dulled by undue involvement in unimportant pastimes. I need your full attention, yes, I need complete dedication.

I am calling all My chosen to put off the self life and to walk in the Spirit. This is not a new message. It was the message of the apostles [and] Jesus. It was also the message of the Psalms and Proverbs, insofar as they emphasize uncompromising loyalty to the truth, and outward actions that are consistent with inward convictions.

from *Progress of Another Pilgrim*

Be Deaf to the Cry of the Crowd

December 3

Then he passing through the midst of them went his way.
LUKE 4:30

*T*he moment you set your spiritual eye upon the goal I have given you, the bondage of people is broken. You will be able, as Jesus was, to pass through the midst of them and be freed to be about your Father's business. Do not allow yourself to be trapped by the multitude. Your own higher vision will free you, and there is a path in the Spirit, if you walk in it, where there is free motion.

from *On the Highroad of Surrender*

December 4

GENTLENESS

What doth the LORD require of thee, but to do justly, and to love mercy,
and to walk humbly with thy God?
MICAH 6:8

*B*e obedient to My commands: so shall I bless you. Let Me guide you: thus shall you know the right path. Follow always the call of the Spirit. All who listen shall hear. Move with the flexibility of a yielded will. Mercies are laid up in store for the humble.

Gentleness of spirit brings overcoming power. It is not the strong will, but the yielded will that is blessed in My sight.

from *Progress of Another Pilgrim*

December 5

SAFETY IN GOD'S WILL

If any man be a worshipper of God, and doeth his will, him he heareth.
JOHN 9:31

*M*y will is not a place, but a condition. You will discover blessing in every place, and any place, if your spirit is in tune with Me.

I direct every motion of your life, as the ocean bears a ship. Your will and intelligence may be at the helm, but divine providence and sovereignty are stronger forces.

Move on steadily, and know that the waters that carry you are the waters of My love and My kindness, and I will keep you on the right course.

from *Come Away My Beloved*

I Control the Winds

Guide our feet into the way of peace.
LUKE 1:79

*M*y child, do not be dismayed by any calamity that befalls you. Never doubt My care. Never question My dealings. I am leading you by the narrowness of the way. It is often a difficult and precipitous path; but I would assure you of My hand of protection.

Put your life in My hands, and it will be for you a place of peace and of spiritual comfort. So long as you abide in this place, I will control the rains that fall upon you and the winds that blow.

from *Come Away My Beloved*

_____

_____

_____

_____

_____

Mercy

December 7

Love ye your enemies. . . . Be ye therefore merciful,
as your Father also is merciful.
LUKE 6:35–36

*M*ercy is the extension of My grace. Whenever you show mercy to another, you express My love. I rejoice in forgiveness. I do not give grudgingly. You have been told to give cheerfully of your substance; now I say unto you, do the same in the Spirit. Do not question and do not delay.

Deal justly, but in patience and understanding, and add not evil upon evil. As I have given to you, so likewise do you to others.

from *On the Highroad of Surrender*

_____

_____

_____

_____

_____

EXERCISE YOUR FAITH

They went forth, and preached every where, the Lord working with them.
MARK 16:20

*E*xercise your faith, knowing that I will give you the right words and will fill them with the power of My Spirit, and they shall be used by Me to bring salvation and deliverance.

Be not detained by self-doubt. Rely on Me, and do not regard your own limitations as a liability.

I will manifest through you in a mighty way if you will only give Me the opportunity. Be My mouthpiece, and I will supply the words and the message.

from *Progress of Another Pilgrim*

INNER COMMUNION

*Whosoever shall not receive you, nor hear you, when ye depart thence,
shake off the dust under your feet for a testimony against them.*
MARK 6:11

*W*hen I place upon your ministry the seal of Mine approval it shall no longer be important to you whether or not you are accepted by any other.

We are co-laborers together—I and you and the Father. Keep a strong awareness of this identification. You will lose the anointing if you allow anyone to enter and distract.

Stay in the holy place of inner communion and I will break forth through your vessel.

from *Progress of Another Pilgrim*

DISAPPOINTMENT

No man, having put his hand to the plough, and looking back,
is fit for the kingdom of God.
LUKE 9:62

*O*ut of every disappointment there is to be gleaned some treasure. The enemy would whisper "all is lost." I say to you, much can be gained.

Refuse the temptation to brood over what is gone. It has passed into the area of My sovereignty. The present challenge requires your undivided attention.

Give no time to dark thoughts. Depression undermines the vigor of the soul.

from *On the Highroad of Surrender*

THE POWER OF HOLINESS

December 11

Greater is he that is in you, than he that is in the world.
1 JOHN 4:4

*T*he devil does not seek to destroy the vile person so much as the holy one. All hell trembles when God's prophet takes command in the Name of Jesus over evil powers. This is the man who is hated by the adversary. I will give My servant power to stand, and he shall know that his own soul is being preserved by the very power of holiness within him, which is My own Spirit, the true objective of the enemy.

from *On the Highroad of Surrender*

HIDDEN RESOURCES

We glory in tribulations also: knowing that tribulation worketh patience.
ROMANS 5:3

December 12

*A*ccept the trials of life as they come, and look for the good in each. Only in this way can you advance and grow in stature.

It is only through the power of My Spirit within you that you shall be able to tap hidden resources that have power to sustain you above yourself. Therefore you are not dependent upon nor limited by the level of your own strength of character, but you may rise above it and lift your own actions up into My divine pattern for you.

from *Progress of Another Pilgrim*

December 13

MIGHTY TRIUMPH

He that heareth my word, and believeth on him that sent me,
hath everlasting life.
JOHN 5:24

*T*he present conflict shall be counted trivial in the light of the mighty triumph that is to come. For they shall stand before Me to be judged: but he that believeth in the Son hath everlasting life, and shall not come into condemnation, but is passed already from death into life. These who believe shall reign with Me, yea, they shall judge both men and angels.

Make this present moment one of victory in Me.

from *Dialogues with God*

Exalt His Name

In the beginning. . .the Word was with God. . . .
All things were made by him.
JOHN 1:1, 3

*L*et none tell you My Son is as others; lo, He is the Son of God, yes, He is God the Son. Exalt His Name and rejoice in His majesty; for the heavens were fashioned by His hand, and man is His creation. What man of all earth's personages can lay claim to any such power of creation?

Yes, His works alone shall proclaim His power and deity. Man cannot extinguish the light of His glorious works.

from *Progress of Another Pilgrim*

A Crucial Hour

Watch ye therefore, and pray always, that ye may be accounted worthy
to escape all these things that shall come to pass,
and to stand before the Son of man.
LUKE 21:36

*W*atch for the signs of My soon-coming. No concern lies more heavily on My heart than the preparation of My chosen ones for the ingathering. Not only do you need to prepare your own hearts, but I would use you to warn and help others.

This is no time for apathy. There has been no more crucial hour in all man's history.

from *Progress of Another Pilgrim*

THE ROD AND THE LOOK

Peter remembered the word of the Lord. . . Before the cock crow,
thou shalt deny me thrice. And Peter went out, and wept bitterly.
LUKE 22:61–62

*A*s you come into a closer relationship with Me and the maturity of the walk of the true Bride, I deal with you as a husband who gently remonstrates with his wife, impressing upon her his thoughts and wishes, often with only a look.

Just to draw near Me in a time of failure brings to the sensitive, loving spirit deeper suffering than was ever brought to a disobedient child by the chastening rod.

from *On the Highroad of Surrender*

December 17

RELEASE YOUR GRIEF

Take my yoke upon you and learn of me; for I am meek and lowly in heart:
and ye shall find rest unto your souls.
MATTHEW 11:29

*M*y child, lean your head upon My bosom. I know well your weariness, and every burden I would lift. Never bury your griefs, but offer them up to Me. You will relieve your soul of much strain if you can lay every care in My hand. Never cling to any trouble, hoping to resolve it yourself, but turn it over to Me. In doing so, you will free Me to work it out.

from *Come Away My Beloved*

TRUE HOLINESS

Present your bodies a living sacrifice, holy, acceptable unto God.
ROMANS 12:1

True holiness, when wrought in you by My grace, is not an end in itself. It is a transforming work by the Holy Spirit to the end that My will may be accomplished through you. If you are a flowing, vital part of My eternal purpose, you are blessed.

Stretch forth the hand of faith. Set foot upon the territory you wish to claim. I will clear a path, but you must be determined to follow closely, and to hold your ground without wavering.

from On the Highroad of Surrender

STAY PLIABLE IN MY HAND

I am come that they may have life, and. . .have it more abundantly.
JOHN 10:10

Be quick to obey. Regardless of the cost. You will always be amply repaid for any sacrifice with an abundance of blessing. There will always be an easier way open to you, one that will seem more reasonable, involving less risk. I have calculated the risk to test and develop your faith as well as your obedience, and in the choosing process, I give you an opportunity to prove your love for Me.

Be sensitive to My Spirit.

from Come Away My Beloved

December 20

Victory in Adversity

We know that all things work together for good to them that love God,
to them who are the called according to his purpose.
Romans 8:28

*W*henever you experience pain, know that I am knocking at the door of your heart.

Nothing should be of any real concern to you except your relationship to Me and a right attitude toward others. Life brings unpleasant circumstances, but I say unto you, I am in the midst, causing all experiences, both pleasant and otherwise, to harmonize for your blessing and growth.

I give you victory while in the throes of adversity.

from *On the Highroad of Surrender*

December 21

I Am Everywhere

Heal the sick, cleanse the lepers, raise the dead, cast out devils:
freely ye have received, freely give.
Matthew 10:8

*N*ever flounder on the rocks of indecision. The call of My heart to you is for your utter abandon to the waters of My will. I am everywhere. Think not that any man can shut Me out. Wherever you go you bear the Wind of the Spirit. It shall bring new life into any situation. It shall breathe upon the dead, and they shall live. It shall touch the one who has completely given up with a ray of new courage.

from *Progress of Another Pilgrim*

INATTENTION

Take heed therefore that the light which is in thee be not darkness.
If thy whole body therefore be full of light, having no part dark,
the whole shall be full of light.
LUKE 11:35–36

I am grieved by your hardness of heart and inattention. Open rebellion usually brings immediate punishment. Inattention can be even more destructive to the soul, because it often goes unnoticed and unrepented, and is a secret, unexposed sin.

Cast it out in Jesus' Name, and refuse the robber who would take your dearest treasure: your singleness of heart in your love for Me.

from *On the Highroad of Surrender*

A CONSUMING DESIRE

If I yet pleased men, I should not be the servant of Christ.
GALATIANS 1:10

*I*f I lay not My hand upon you in punishment, come near. Look into My eyes. Dare to draw close to My heart. You will know surely My desire and purpose for you and shall grieve more that you have displeased Me than that you may have forfeited some personal gain or blessing. You will not view your spiritual walk as a challenge to be a successful Christian in the eyes of others, but will have a consuming desire to please Me.

from *On the Highroad of Surrender*

December 24

DESIRE HOLINESS

For sin shall not have dominion over you:
for ye are not under the law, but under grace.
ROMANS 6:14

*Y*ou should never abandon your desire for holiness because of your failures. You judge yourself incurably sinful. I see you as potentially pure. When you can look upon your own soul with compassion, you will know that My spirit has worked a work of grace in your heart, and you shall be lifted above despair. You shall have a song of praise on your lips and a shout of victory in your heart.

from *Make Haste My Beloved*

_____

_____

_____

_____

_____

December 25

THE CROSS IN THE STAR

The Word was made flesh, and dwelt among us, (and we beheld his glory,
the glory as of the only begotten of the Father,) full of grace and truth.
JOHN 1:14

*T*he Cross, My child, is My symbol of Christmas. Wise men followed the star, but it was the Savior whom they sought. Wrapped that holy night in swaddling clothes was My perfect gift to mankind. Cradled in the arms of Mary lay the only hope of human salvation. Shepherds were drawn to worship Him by the love that flowed through Him as He became the channel for redeeming grace.

from *On the Highroad of Surrender*

_____

_____

_____

_____

_____

I Shall Come Singing

*Be ye therefore ready also: for the Son of man cometh
at an hour when ye think not.*
LUKE 12:40

*B*e silent before Me. I will lift up My voice as the sound of a trumpet—I will speak clearly to you, for the hour is at hand. Be obedient. For My face is set toward My imminent return to earth. I wait only the release from the Father's hand. Keep your vision filled with Me. Keep your life in tune and your worship in mutual harmony.

For I will come singing, and what will you be if you are in discord?

from Come Away My Beloved

On Not Resisting Evil

December 27

*Resist not evil: but whosoever shall smite thee on thy right cheek,
turn to him the other also.*
MATTHEW 5:39

*M*y wisdom will come to you, My child, when you become quiet. Anxiety places the soul in stress. The strivings of your own heart will be as out of harmony with My Spirit as the evil you wish to combat. This is why the Scripture says, "Resist not evil."

You cannot correct the crooked path of another, but you can let Me show you how to make a straight path of your own. Never fear the darkness. . .avoid it.

from On the Highroad of Surrender

COUNSEL WITH ME

God hath given them the spirit of slumber, eyes that they should not see,
and ears that they should not hear.
ROMANS 11:8

*B*e not disturbed by evildoers. They are in My hand to do as I please, even as are the righteous. All is under My control. Stand upon My Word, and let your only support be your faith in Me.

What goes on in the lives of others need not distress you. I will deal with them. Walk in Me. Counsel with Me, and look to Me alone for your direction and your encouragement.

from *Progress of Another Pilgrim*

INTEGRITY A SACRED CHARGE

Do all to the glory of God.
1 CORINTHIANS 10:31

*T*here is a way that you must go because of faithfulness to Me. All you do, let it be as unto Me. Never do anything as pleasing men, but do all for Me and for My glory. Thus, and only thus, can your heart be kept at peace, and only in this way can you honor Me and bring forth fruit.

Speak of Me often, and all other relationships shall be hallowed.

The integrity of your own heart is your most sacred charge. Guard this with utmost care.

from *Progress of Another Pilgrim*

THE SHADOW OF MY HAND

*Peace I leave with you, my peace I give unto you:
not as the world giveth, give I unto you.*
JOHN 14:27

*P*eace, My child, is the shadow of My hand. When your soul is at rest, it is because you are consciously aware of My presence. You do not need to seek peace. As you realize My nearness, you will discover that I am there, in the center of your worship; for to seek Me is to desire to worship Me. Finding Me, you have no need to seek peace, for I Myself am your peace.

from *On the Highroad of Surrender*

THE LAST GREAT OUTPOURING

December 31

I am Alpha and Omega, the beginning and the ending, saith the Lord.
REVELATION 1:8

I have truly great things in store for you. I will send a mighty downpour. In the day of the great deluge which is coming, many will come to know the reality of My power.

Surely I will pour out My Spirit, I will reaffirm the veracity of My Word and bring the message of the Gospel of Redemption to many who would otherwise never give heed. I am the Alpha and the Omega. Stand firm in Me. Never waver.

from *Come Away My Beloved*

INDEX

53:3—4/20
55:8—2/18
55:11—3/22
57:21—2/25
58:11—3/8
59:19—3/14

Jeremiah
2:13—3/30
10:23—6/30
33:3—2/14

Lamentations
3:22–23—8/10

Ezekiel
1:16—3/19
46:15—5/31

Daniel
2:22—1/21
3:25—3/10
3:27—3/11
4:37—2/12
6:22—2/23
11:32—2/21

Hosea
5:15—7/21
6:3—5/8

Joel
2:1—9/1
3:13—5/30

Amos
3:7—5/24
8:11—8/17

Micah
6:8—12/4

Malachi
4:2—6/20

Matthew
5:7—4/15
5:8—11/26
5:13—5/5
5:39—12/27
6:6—5/3
6:28–29—11/5
6:33—9/12
6:34—10/17
7:14—10/23
8:22—7/26
9:29—8/16
10:8—12/21
10:30—7/23
11:28—4/17, 8/15
11:29—12/17
12:36—10/2
12:37—10/1

13:12—2/5
13:39—11/9
14:29—9/9
16:25—4/19
16:26—10/9
17:21—9/15
19:17—9/19
23:11—5/29
23:25—10/12
25:29—3/23

Mark
1:22, 34–35—4/22
4:22—8/8
4:24—8/7
5:19—11/11
6:11—12/9
6:31—6/15
6:35–36—12/7
8:35—4/3, 11/8
8:38—6/17
11:24—4/26
16:15—8/25
16:20—9/8, 12/8

Luke
1:41—12/1
1:53—5/23
1:79—12/6
4:30—12/3
5:4—11/14
6:35–36—12/7

6:38—7/3
6:42—11/12
6:44—11/10
8:18—11/7
9:62—9/7, 12/10
10:1—6/13
10:2—6/11
10:19—10/14
10:41–42—11/23
11:35–36—12/22
12:32—10/13
12:40—6/21, 12/26
14:33—11/29
18:17—10/18
18:22—10/15
21:36—12/15
22:61–62—12/16

John
1:1, 3—12/14
1:14—12/25
4:14—1/24
4:14—2/11, 10/26
5:4—7/20
5:24—8/29, 12/13
6:51—11/30
9:31—12/5
10:10—12/19
13:17—12/2
14:6—11/24
14:12—7/15
14:21—8/13, 10/31

6/3, 6/4, 6/5, 6/8, 6/10, 6/11, 6/14, 6/24, 6/26, 6/29, 7/2, 7/7, 7/9, 7/12, 7/16, 7/18, 7/19, 7/22, 8/1, 8/3, 8/6, 8/7, 8/9, 8/10, 8/13, 8/14, 8/15, 8/20, 8/23, 8/26, 8/27, 8/28, 8/31, 9/1, 9/7, 9/15, 9/16, 9/19, 9/22, 9/25, 9/29, 10/4, 10/5, 10/6, 10/8, 10/9, 10/12, 10/14, 10/19, 10/21, 10/22, 10/24, 10/25, 11/2, 11/7, 11/8, 11/13, 11/20, 11/24, 11/25, 11/28, 12/3, 12/7, 12/10, 12/11, 12/16, 12/18, 12/20, 12/22, 12/23, 12/25, 12/27, 12/30

Progress of Another Pilgrim

1/4, 1/6, 1/7, 1/8, 1/11, 1/12, 1/15, 1/17, 1/24, 1/27, 2/4, 2/8, 2/15, 2/16, 2/20, 2/23, 2/24, 2/25, 2/29, 3/7, 3/10, 3/12, 3/16, 3/20, 3/23, 3/24, 3/25, 4/7, 4/14, 4/15, 4/16, 4/25, 4/29, 4/30, 5/4, 5/6, 5/8, 5/13, 5/16, 5/18, 5/24, 5/30, 5/31, 6/1, 6/7, 6/9, 6/12, 6/13, 6/16, 6/18, 6/22, 6/23, 6/25, 6/27, 6/28, 6/30, 7/1, 7/4, 7/6, 7/13, 7/14, 7/17, 7/20, 7/25, 7/26, 7/29, 7/30, 8/5, 8/22, 8/24, 8/30, 9/4, 9/6, 9/8, 9/10, 9/11, 9/14, 9/17, 9/18, 9/20, 9/21, 9/24, 9/27, 9/28, 10/1, 10/2, 10/10, 10/15, 10/16, 10/18, 10/20, 10/27, 10/28, 10/29, 10/30, 11/1, 11/5, 11/9, 11/11, 11/15, 11/18, 11/19, 11/21, 11/23, 11/29, 11/30, 12/2, 12/4, 12/8, 12/9, 12/12, 12/14, 12/15, 12/21, 12/28, 12/29